I0458774

Deeper Than You Think

A Biblical Guide to Sexual Purity and Intimacy with God

By: Gloria D. Miller

Hardcover ISBN: 978-1-955579-18-6
Softcover ISBN: 978-1-955579-17-9

This book contains material protected under International and Federal Copyright Laws and Treaties. Any unauthorized reprint or use of this material is prohibited.

Publishing in the United States of America

Publisher: Luminous Publishing

http://www.luminouspublishing.com

For bulk orders or other inquiries, email:

info@luminouspublishing.com

Foreword

In a world inundated with messages that often challenge our values and beliefs, it is a privilege to introduce "A Closer Look at Sexual Purity." I believe this much needed book for the times we're in will serve as a guiding light for those on a journey of faith, growth and development all while navigating the intricate paths of today's society.

Sexual purity is one of those topics that, in our modern era, often evokes mixed emotions, yet it remains at the core of our Christian values. Within these pages, you will discover a compassionate, comprehensive and personal exploration of purity, one that reaches beyond the surface and dives deep into the heart of this vital aspect of Christian life.

Gloria eloquently and skillfully shares her personal journey of sexual purity. It Is Possible! This journey isn't shared from a self-righteous standpoint but from an exposing place of love for her generation. The wisdom, faith, and insights revealed on each page will resonate with the heart and life of each reader. By embracing both the scriptural foundation and practical wisdom shared within these chapters, you will find strength to face the challenges of our time, while upholding the timeless principles of purity and holiness found in the scriptures.

As you embark on this journey through "A Closer Look at Sexual Purity," may you be inspired, encouraged, and equipped to live a life that unequivocally reflects the kind of life that Jesus admonishes us to live. This book is destined to be a sought-after resource for individuals, families, and communities who seek to understand, embrace, and practice the principles of sexual purity in a world that often confuses the boundaries of love and desire.

I encourage you to read with an open heart, a willing spirit, and a desire to grow in your understanding of what it really means to live a life of sexual purity, not as an imposition, but as a pathway to experiencing the fullness of God's grace and love.

It is possible to be sexually pure... someone once said, a fool doesn't learn from his mistakes, a wise man learns from his mistakes and a wiser man learns from the wisdom of others.

Acknowledgments

I am grateful to everyone who provided support with this book. Firstly, I thank God for instructing me to write this book and for giving me the insight and wisdom found in this book. I want to thank my mother, Charita Miller, who encouraged me to write the book when it was just an idea. She also read the first draft of my book and provided constructive feedback. I would also like to thank my father, Dennis Miller, who provided encouragement and insight during this book production process.

My friend Brittany LaBelle was excited about this book from the moment I told her about it. I am grateful for her encouraging words, the gracious feedback she provided on the first draft of the book, and the video review she made after reading the first draft.

I am also grateful for another dear friend, Shabethany Sawyer, who provided meticulous feedback after reading the first draft of this book. I sincerely appreciate her genuine, thought-provoking feedback.

I am incredibly thankful for my pastor, Dr. Cleopatra Williams, who met with me when I was uncertain about whether God truly wanted me to write a book about sexual purity. She encouraged me to write the book and provided me with keen insight that motivated me to complete the book as quickly as possible.

I also thank my church family at Life Changers Ministries International. The church's business and economic empowerment ministries held a pitch night for people to pitch their business ideas to receive funding. I pitched my book that night and received funding for publishing.

I am also grateful to Karolyne Roberts and the Luminous Publishing team, who assisted with the publication of this book. I want to thank Victoria Johnson, who provided exceptional insight into the developmental edits.

A special thank you to my godmother, Bishop Gloria Redd, who encouraged and prayed for me throughout this book production process. I am also thankful for Chad Allen's feedback on different aspects of my book. I appreciate how Chad Allen's Book Camp community provides valuable tips, motivation, and encouragement for authors.

Table of Contents

"Honor marriage, and guard the sacredness of sexual intimacy between wife and husband. God draws a firm line against casual and illicit sex" (Hebrews 13:4 MSG).

Introduction

Some of you have picked up this book because you desire to have a pure lifestyle devoid of any sort of immoral act. Others possibly picked it up because they heard that Christians should be sexually pure, but are unsure of whether they are still pure or if they can remain pure. On the other hand, there is someone out there who may think that it is absurd or even impossible for someone to be abstinent and so, decided to explore this book out of sheer curiosity. Whatever your reason for embarking on this journey is, I pray that this book blesses and enhances your life.

First Corinthians 1:17 can beautifully describe my purpose for writing this book. It says, "God didn't send me out to collect a following for myself, but to preach the message of what He has done, collecting a following for Him. And He didn't send me to do it with a lot of fancy rhetoric of my own, lest the powerful action at the center—Christ on the Cross—be trivialized into mere words." I did not write this book to condemn but to enlighten and encourage. I pray that beyond these words, you will feel just that.

I have been passionate about sexual purity for some time now. I have always felt like it was a topic that was not elaborated upon much in church. I remember sitting in a church service one day, and a preacher passionately mentioned that Christians should not have sex outside of marriage; then, he moved on to his next point. At that moment, I asked God why preachers do not usually explain how you can successfully practice abstinence. The Lord responded by saying many of these preachers can't share tips because they weren't abstinent before marriage. How can you share what you don't know?

This revelation from God provided understanding and insight into why many preachers do not dive deeper into how you can maintain sexual purity before marriage. It also made me concerned for all the unmarried people who hear that they should not have sex before marriage but are unable to do this because they don't know how. Because of that explanation, I became even more determined to write this book and share all the information on sexual purity I had accumulated during my 30 years of virginity.

I believe many Christians are losing the battle to be sexually pure because they do not have the proper strategies. It's like baking cookies for the first time without a recipe. You can be extremely passionate and desire those cookies, but you will not be successful without a recipe or some prior knowledge of baking cookies. I wrote this book so people could have a recipe for sexual purity. It is my desire for people to build stronger relationships with God as a result of their purity journey.

I attended a Christian school for most of my childhood and adolescence. At age five, I gave my life to Christ during a service at school. At that age, I thought being saved involved believing in Jesus Christ and being obedient to my authority figures. I did not have a deep relationship with God where I spent time with Him and tried to truly walk in His will for my life until I was in college. Joyce Meyer had a 30-day Bible study challenge that I did while in college. This helped me to build the rhythm of having a quiet time with God and journaling, and this resulted in me growing closer to God. I continued to study the Bible even after the 30 days ended.

During my 7th, 8th, and 9th-grade years, various speakers came to my school and spoke about abstaining from sex until marriage. During this season, God gave me the desire to remain a virgin until marriage. When I made the decision, I did not realize how difficult the journey would be. There were temptations, doubts about whether God desired for Christians to be sexually pure, and moments where I wanted to give up simply because I wanted to fit in and was curious about what sex felt like. However, if I can be sexually pure, then you can do it, too, even if you've had sex before. So do not give up on this journey. It is so worth it! I am grateful that God has kept me all of these years. I am still a virgin because of His grace, strength, and guidance. It is my prayer that I remain a virgin until I am married.

Before we even begin discussing sexual purity, I think it's important to reflect on Psalm 37:4. This verse says, "Delight yourself also, in the Lord, and He shall give you the desires of your heart." This scripture verse has been interpreted in different ways, but I believe it means that God's desires become your desires when you delight in Him. Deciding to have a lifestyle of purity is a desire that is developed once you delight in the Lord. According to the Merriam-Webster dictionary, "delight" means "to take keen pleasure," "to give keen enjoyment," or "to give joy or satisfaction to." If you have never truly obtained pleasure from the Lord, I implore you to try this today. Ask the Holy Spirit to help you find absolute joy and delight in the Lord, and watch how you begin to form new desires!

I pray that you grow in your understanding of the importance of purity in your life and relationship with God. I hope that by reading this book, you realize that although sexual purity can be a serious struggle, it is attainable.

Chapter 1:

What is Purity?

How would you feel if I told you that sexual purity is God's will for your life and everyone else on this planet? Don't be disappointed if you didn't know. God's will for our lives has different facets, and sexual purity is one of them. First Thessalonians 4:3 says, *"God's will is for you to be holy, so stay away from sexual sin."*

Many people want to know God's will in some areas of their lives, but not all. For example, many people want to know God's will concerning their mate, education, or career, but they do not even bother to ask God's will for their sex life or daily habits.

I like to think of myself as a miracle virgin. I know it can seem like a miracle for anyone to be a virgin at a certain age because it is common for people to lose their virginity when they are teenagers or in their early twenties.

I think I'm a miracle virgin because I knew I wanted to wait until marriage to have sex for the first time. However, I did not understand what would be required to remain a virgin. (I also did not think I would be single this long, but that's another book for another day.) I had no idea how deep sexual purity was and the true extent of the commitment to be sexually abstinent. I knew what I was supposed to do. However, I did not know how to do it.

I was a virgin who masturbated occasionally, watched whatever I wanted to watch (no matter how raunchy), and listened to whatever I wanted to listen to. I had no fundamental in-depth understanding of purity. I heard about it in the Bible and thought I understood it, but I didn't. I HAD NO CLUE WHAT

PURITY WAS. It's both funny and scary, to be honest. Sexual purity is a lot deeper than I thought it was back then.

I strongly desired to visit a strip club during my first year of college. I had no idea why I wanted to go so badly. I was never a party or club person. I spent weekend evenings watching movies, hanging out with friends, or doing homework. But that desire was so strong that I ended up telling my friends I wanted to go to a male strip club for my birthday. They found one, and we planned to go for my birthday.

As I reflect on that time, I think I wanted to go to the strip club so badly because it seemed fun. When I watched movies or shows where people went to strip clubs, it appeared like they were having a lot of fun. I am also a heterosexual woman, so watching men with incredible bodies dance around would satisfy my fleshly desires. However, my flesh would only be temporarily satisfied. Eventually, I would have to find more ways to meet the desires of my flesh.

The strip club plan was halted by a conviction I received while watching a sermon. During my first year of college, I watched church on Sundays online, and one Sunday, I watched a sermon by Joyce Meyer. She was talking about being disciplined and to whom much is given; much is required. She elaborated on how Christians should be disciplined about what they watch, listen to, where they go, etc. I felt so convicted. I never thought about how everything I did affect my spiritual life.

Well, that day, I decided to change my lifestyle. I decided to be more selective about what I watched, where I went, and the music I listened to. I also decided to tell my friends that I did not want to go to a strip club for my birthday anymore. They were disappointed but respected my decision. I know they didn't understand. They may have even thought I was lame, but I was more concerned about pleasing God than getting people to think I was cool.

Do you want to know what else? IT FELT GOOD! It felt good on the inside to please God. Yes, my flesh wasn't happy. My flesh was having a tough time. However, my heart was glad. I had tremendous inner peace. Slowly but surely, I began learning about purity and pursuing it more intensely. I can't believe I'm telling you ALL my business.

Many people believe that purity is an unnecessary concept that religious people practice and discuss. Many believe their lives are hard enough as it is, so they do not desire the addition of purity, further complicating life. Besides, some of these impure things help people to relax and keep their minds off the stresses of life. However, according to the dictionary, purity IS freedom. The New Oxford American Dictionary defines purity as:

1. Freedom from adulteration or contamination
2. Freedom from immorality, especially of a sexual nature.

From this definition, it is evident that your purity is connected to your freedom.

What do you need freedom from? What do you personally run to when you feel freedom is not your portion? What is weighing you down? What is bringing unnecessary stress into your life? What are you doing to cope or eliminate the stress that is displeasing to God? People make many attempts to solve their stress issues with coping mechanisms that only bring moments of temporary happiness.

Are you searching for true joy? Then start pursuing purity through Jesus Christ. You can begin to do that today by talking with a trusted Christian friend about things you have been struggling with. You can also watch sermons and other Christian content online, read the Bible, seek God's help through prayer, and intentionally listen for His guidance.

The world cannot teach us how to be truly pure. The Bible calls us to "*Put to death, therefore, whatever belongs to your earthly nature:*

sexual immorality, impurity, lust, evil desires, and greed, which is idolatry" (Colossians 3:5). If you want to obtain true freedom through having a lifestyle of purity, you must follow the most remarkable human example of purity, Jesus Christ.

Purity is defined as "freedom from adulteration…" I want to dig deeper into the word "adulteration." It is the noun form of the verb adulterate. According to the New Oxford American Dictionary, adulterate means to "render (something) poorer in quality by adding another substance, typically an inferior one." The word "adulteration" describes reducing food quality by adding hazardous chemicals.

According to James 1:18, we are the first fruits of God. We adulterate ourselves when we add things to our lives that are inferior to the standard that God has set for us. You can adulterate yourself by adding inferior friends, food, beverages, drugs, habits, songs, shows, movies, clothing, thinking patterns, activities, etc., to your life.

The songs I listened to used to be a significant area of adulteration in my life. When I was younger, I listened to anything that sounded good, even if I disagreed with the lyrics. As I grew in my Christian walk, I realized how much the lyrics disagreed with the Word of God.

I became annoyed at some of the lyrics and realized that these songs were feeding lies to me and possibly millions of others. I also noticed how these lyrics impacted my thought patterns and how I saw the world. So one day, I did a major playlist cleanup and deleted all the songs I no longer wanted to be fed into my spirit.

Many of these songs promoted sex outside marriage, promiscuity, vanity, material possessions, and valuing physical appearance more than other personal qualities. These songs were a source of adulteration because they distracted me from the values and lifestyle that God desired for me to have. They promoted a lifestyle that contradicts the lifestyle a Christian should have.

First Samuel 16:7 clearly shows us what God values in a person. The NKJV says, "*...For the Lord does not see as man sees; for man looks at the outward appearance, but the Lord looks at the heart.*" This verse alone makes it clear that the values portrayed in the songs I was listening to were not in line with the values God deems important.

Sometimes, people adulterate themselves without even knowing it. Negative thoughts are "rotten" things with which people adulterate themselves without even knowing. For a very long time, I was not looking forward to marriage. I struggled with the idea that marriages are unreliable. I thought that even if I got married one day, it would end in heartbreak and divorce. Who looks forward to difficult times and heartbreak?

Growing up, I knew of people who got divorced and people who were in miserable marriages. I was not close to anyone with a happy, healthy marriage that I could see as an example. I always had the mindset that I needed to be able to support myself financially because even if I got married one day, things might not work out, and I could be on my own. Isn't that sad?

I did not have a strong desire to get married. I can't tell you the exact moment this negative mindset about marriage changed, but as I grew in my walk with God and consumed content where people talked about their healthy marriages, I started to gain hope in marriage. Now I have a more optimistic view of romantic relationships. My trust in God also grew, and I believe God will bless me with a healthy marriage that lasts until my future husband or I die.

Ephesians 4:22-24 says, "*...everything—and I do mean everything—connected with that old way of life has to go. It's rotten through and through. Get rid of it! And then take on an entirely new* *way of life—a God-fashioned life, a life renewed from the inside and working itself into your conduct as God accurately reproduces his character in you."*

I pray that adulteration ceases in your life this instant and from this day forward, you only add things of superior quality to your life. May God grant you the wisdom to discern His standards so you can differentiate between the inferior and the superior. I pray that the bonds of inferiority be broken in your life in the name of Jesus Christ. If you have never heard this before, I want you to know that God created you for the superior, not the inferior. Stop adulterating yourself by settling.

I do not want you to think that obtaining purity is super easy and second nature. Nor do I want you to feel condemned for the impure parts of your life. Contamination is already within us, so we must put in the hard work and discipline to become pure with the help of the Holy Spirit. Obtaining purity is not something that we can accomplish on our own. We need the Holy Spirit to guide us through this lifelong process.

While talking to a crowd one day, Jesus mentioned, *"For from within, out of a person's heart, come evil thoughts, sexual immorality, theft, murder, adultery, greed, wickedness, deceit, lustful desires, envy, slander, pride, and foolishness. All these vile things come from within; they are what defile you"* (Mark 7:21-23). God is fully aware of the deceit within us when He calls us to have pure lives. Therefore, He gave us the Holy Spirit and the Bible to guide us through decontamination.

The things we add when we adulterate only expose or awaken the impurity that is already within. When we adulterate, we make the situation worse. Instead of growing towards purity, we shrink away from it. Second Corinthians 7:1 calls us to *"cleanse ourselves from all filthiness of the flesh and spirit, perfecting holiness in the fear of God."* Sometimes we cleanse ourselves of some filthiness, but not all because we have grown accustomed to some of our filth. I encourage you to be obedient to God's word and thoroughly cleanse yourself of filthiness.

Take a moment to consider the things that are filthy in your life. What are some areas that you need to clean up? Write down some of these areas and plan how to rid yourself of them.

Remember to give yourself grace during your lifelong purification process. Getting rid of all the impurities will not happen overnight. Becoming entirely pure is a process that has multiple layers. So do not give up if you notice that you continue to fall into the same sin patterns, although you are trying to stop.

Proverbs 24:16 says, "*...for the righteous falls seven times and rises again...*" You will fall; nobody is exempt from that. However, it would be best if you got back up. Reward yourself for your little progress and continue building on that progress. Obtaining purity is a step-by-step process. When practicing purity, you're not simply fighting the flesh; there is a spiritual battle as well.

Purity should not be confused with perfection. I think many people try not to attain purity because they feel like it is impossible. God calls us to live pure lifestyles, and we are gifted with the Holy Spirit, who serves as a helper in this effort. It is possible to be pure and not perfect. The New Oxford American Dictionary defines perfect as "having all the required or desirable elements, qualities, or characteristics; as good as it is possible to be." You can have a pure heart and be free from adulteration, contamination, and immorality but still not be perfect.

Pure characteristics and perfect characteristics can be completely different. There is a difference between having a title and truly being set apart. You may know someone who has the qualities of a perfect teacher because they are intelligent, patient, kind, and able to explain things exceptionally well. But bear in mind that just because this person has the qualities of a perfect teacher does not mean that they would be a pure teacher. To determine whether they would be a pure teacher, you would have to know their heart's posture and determine whether they are free from adulteration, contamination, or immorality.

The world does not seem to care very much about purity but is driven toward what it considers perfection. However, what the world considers perfection is very different from the biblical standards. This is because the qualities that God wants you to embody are vastly different from the qualities that the secular world prioritizes.

People are driven toward achieving accomplishments and perfecting things, so they are the best at what they do. However, the same amount of effort is not placed into being pure in what they do. One might dare to say that purity is not valuable in society. Therefore, some of the most impure people have achieved outstanding accomplishments and are admired most in society. However, some pure people have not accomplished much according to the world's standards. Therefore, people do not regard them highly or ignore them.

As believers, we must stop and reflect on the condition of our hearts. We should think about our motives, whom we are striving to impress ultimately, and why their opinions matter. Are you truly free from adulteration, contamination, and immorality? Is your heart genuinely pure and pleasing to God? As Christians, we should aim for purity in every area of our lives. This makes life significantly easier and less stressful.

Chapter 2:

Pure Actions

To explore the definition of purity further, I want to briefly touch on pure actions. James 1:27 says, "Pure and undefiled religion before God and the Father is this: to visit orphans and widows in their trouble, and to keep oneself unspotted from the world." One way we can practice purity is to help those in need. Be there for someone going through a hard time instead of only worrying about yourself all the time.

Many people struggle to be pure when interacting with people in their everyday lives. When we often describe someone's behavior as rude, we are saying that their actions are impure. For instance, if someone refers to another person by a negative or derogatory term, this can be considered an impure action. On the other hand, the pure action would be to refer to them by a positive or uplifting term.

Sometimes, people's actions can be impure when they act according to their feelings. For example, if someone is insulted, they tend to respond by insulting the person who offended them even more. Being insulted or hurt does not validate impure actions, especially if you are a Christian. Christians are called to die to their flesh with the help of the Holy Spirit. The pure response would be to pray and forgive the insulting person.

In that same example of responding to insulting people, if the person responded with an insult, the situation could escalate into a heated argument where both individuals are angry, hurt, and resentful. However, by reacting purely, the Christian can win over the insulting person (if they are not saved already). Or, if the person is saved, they could learn more about practicing forgiveness and purity. This would result in them becoming stronger Christians and building their character.

One great piece of advice for having pure actions is to involve the Holy Spirit before you act, especially if you are emotional about a situation. You cannot carry out this purity journey alone, no matter how long you have been saved. Someone may have mastered purity in one area but still needs to develop it in other areas of their lives. Displaying pure actions will become easier as you continue the practice of involving the Holy Spirit in your decisions before you act. In a matter of time, acting impurely would not even be a thought that comes into your head.

James 1:27 also describes purity as *"keeping oneself unspotted from the world."* Later on in this book, I will go into more detail about how we can limit worldly influence in the area of sex. However, contamination with the ideologies and practices of the world can be controlled by being cautious of the people you spend a lot of time with, filtering the songs you listen to or the shows you watch, and being intentional about enhancing your spiritual life.

The people you spend time with can greatly influence your outlook on life and your desire to be pure. Be sure that the people you spend most of your time with are also pursuing purity. You will know this by their fruit. If your circle of friends produces impure or no fruit at all, you should seriously consider finding a new circle of friends. This may be tough at first, especially if you have been friends with these people for a long time and built bonds. Be encouraged that God created us to live in community with others and that He will send you friends who can be pure influences.

Often, people think they can listen or watch anything because they know their standards and values. Sometimes the media can influence people subconsciously. Their thinking makes minor changes, and their value system undergoes a substantial shift after a while.

I used to watch some reality shows where the stars had no form of Godliness. No drastic changes happened immediately, but as time progressed, I realized that my mindset was beginning to shift. I started to put significantly more value into the physical than the internal and even desired unnecessary things that would not truly benefit my life. I also noticed that I was losing respect for men because a lot of the men on these shows were unfaithful to their significant others.

I had an "aha moment" after the Holy Spirit brought these things to my attention, and I decided to filter the songs, movies, and shows I allowed to minister to me. Over time, I noticed my mindset shifting more toward Christ. It was challenging and very tempting because the songs, movies, and shows were entertaining, but I had to remind myself of my ultimate life goal of honoring God with my life. I also had the help of the Holy Spirit.

To be completely honest, the more time you spend listening to songs, watching movies, and watching shows that sow impure seeds, the less time you have to consume the things of God. You cannot be filled up with the things of Christ because the things of this world have already taken up so much space within you. Also, because you spend more time consuming impure things, they become more deeply rooted than Christ-like things. So, the Christ-like seeds do not have a chance to take root and produce the godly character you need to thrive spiritually.

Seeds that cannot take root end up dying. Since the Christ-like seeds die, the only seeds left are the impure seeds. The impure seeds become deeply rooted over time, so they are the main influencers of your actions. The actions influenced by impure roots will not be pure, so you find yourself constantly repenting.

You may decide to filter the things that you let into your spirit. This is good, but you would have to go through the process of deliverance, where you remove the impure seeds that have taken root within you and replace them with pure, Christ-like seeds. The Bible calls us to *"be renewed in the spirit of [our] mind"* (Ephesians 4:23). If this process is skipped, you will find yourself constantly having inner battles. This can be detrimental to your Christian walk because you may begin to feel hopeless and think you cannot achieve a pure Christian life.

I pray that God helps you display pure actions. I also pray that He shows you the people or habits you need to get rid of so you can live in true purity. May the Holy Spirit guide you throughout the day so your actions can be pure, even when faced with temptations. Believe that you can display pure actions even if you have a track record of acting contrary to the word of God.

Chapter 3:

Pure Motives

Not every pure act has pure motives behind it. Proverbs 16:2 touches on having pure motives. It says, *"All a person's ways seem pure to them, but motives are weighed by the Lord."* God is the ultimate judge of purity. I had impure motives for years. I did not realize that my motives were impure until God pointed them out to me.

For a long time, I was friendly to people and very helpful simply because I had rejection issues and wanted people to approve of me. This mode of operation does not line up with the Word of God, which states, *"Am I now trying to win the approval of human beings, or of God? Or am I trying to please people? If I were still trying to please people, I would not be a servant of Christ"* (Galatians 1:10).

Being nice to people for approval worked; people liked me because I was so lovely and compliant. One day, when I was feeling overwhelmed, God asked me why I had agreed to help with something that I had committed to. It was then that I realized I had not agreed to this act of kindness simply because I wanted to help, but I sought approval from people. My ways seemed pure to me, but at that moment, God weighed my motives right in front of me.

First Timothy 1:5 says, *"The purpose of my instruction is that all believers would be filled with love that comes from a pure heart, a clear conscience, and genuine faith."* Why do you do the good deeds that you do? Are your motives truly pure? Are you being nice to that friend, teacher, professor, coworker, boss, or church leader because you believe it will help you advance in life or because you genuinely care about their well-being? In the end, God is the ultimate judge of your motives.

Discernment is a great way to detect whether motives are pure. Ask the Holy Spirit to show you when your motives or someone else's motives are not pure. When determining whether another person's motives are pure, listen out for keywords or phrases that would indicate the reason behind their actions. You will be surprised at how the person reveals their true motive without even realizing it.

Another indicator of impure motives can be seen when people are excessive in their acts of kindness. A classic example of this is when a male meets an attractive female, and they shower her with expensive gifts because they are looking for something in return. Sometimes God can indeed send people into your life to bless you more than you ever expected. Therefore, it is good to be prayerful and use discernment.

Patience is also essential when determining the motives behind a person's actions. Someone with impure motives will give up when they do not get what they want. You will see their true motives over time. Do not make any sudden decisions, but watch them to see the type of fruit they truly have. Pure-looking fruits that are produced from impure motives are usually hollow. The fruit looks good and healthy on the outside, but once you remove that outer layer, you realize there is nothing on the inside.

People can keep up the pretenses or that outer layer of fruit for so long, but once you start to bite into that fruit, you realize that there is nothing there. The seemingly pure fruit is hollow. True love, joy, peace, patience, kindness, gentleness, goodness, faithfulness, and long-suffering are not there. People with impure fruit tend to quit once things become complicated.

To determine whether your motives are pure, do frequent self-checks where you reflect on why you are doing the actions you are doing. Ask the Holy Spirit to reveal any motives that may be impure. If you do realize that you have impure motives, ask the Holy Spirit to cleanse you of the impure motives and replace them with pure motives. Replace the hollow, impure fruit with healthy, pure fruit.

An example of an impure fruit is jealousy, and this can lead to sabotaging the success of others. It is not good to never want to see others succeed. Someone else's success does not mean that you are also not successful. There is room on this earth for many people to flourish. The hollow, impure fruit of jealousy can be replaced with the pure fruit of helping others succeed and being genuinely happy when people thrive.

When reflecting on the purity of your motives, it is good to be aware of your true desires. Titus 2:12 talks about *"denying ungodliness and worldly lusts."* However, we cannot do this if we are unaware of our ungodliness and worldly lusts on the inside. I try to maintain awareness of my desires and goals. In my self-checks, I ask myself if I am doing something just so I can achieve one of my goals or desires.

I also reflect on whether I would continue doing a kind deed if it does not allow me to achieve my personal goal or desire. There is nothing wrong with going after your pure desires and goals. However, you are in error when you are using or manipulating people to achieve your desires or goals.

When reflecting on your motives, it is also good to be aware of your insecurities. Often, we act based on how we view ourselves. I was insecure about how I valued myself; therefore, I needed people to validate the fact that I was valuable. I got excited whenever someone asked for my help because I felt like that meant that they valued me. They could have just been using me, but I did not care. I was so caught up in being used by people that I did not pause to find out how God, my Creator, wanted to use me. The Creator created me for a purpose, and I was more concerned with the purpose that the other created beings gave me.

You know that your motives are pure when your heart posture is in the correct alignment with Christ. When you have sought direction from God and are living a life of obedience to God, then your motives are pure. This heart posture also equips you to discern better when the actions of others are impure because you will have firsthand experience of what someone with a pure heart looks like.

My prayer is that you fervently seek God to find out what He created you to do if you have not already done so. I also pray that you walk in obedience and carry out God's purpose and plan for your life. May you experience heightened discernment so you are not distracted or experience any setbacks to God's plan for your life. May your motives be pure in all you do through the wonderful help of the Holy Spirit.

Chapter 4:

Purity Through Priority (Putting God First)

Pure priorities produce pure people. The Bible further defines purity in Psalm 24:4. This verse says, *those whose hands and hearts are pure, who do not worship idols and never tell lies."* Another way purity can be attained is by not putting anything before God in your life. God should be in the first position. When you start putting other things before God, you make an idol out of those things.

One way to identify the idols in your life is to determine what gives you a sense of identity and value. Many people idolize their jobs, possessions, or people that they feel define them or give them an identity. For instance, many people idolize their jobs because their identity is found in their position. They have a high income and are very respected at their job. They feel that if they lose their jobs, they will become less significant or lose their sense of identity.

Some people find their identity in their social circle or spouse. They would do anything to keep these people in their lives. If they ever lost these people, they would feel incomplete, insignificant, and irrecoverable.

Your identity should be in God, not in man or material things. Everything and everyone in your life could vanish in a second, but God is constant. He is a magnificent Heavenly Father, and Christ is an excellent example of how we should live our lives. Because God is your Creator, it only makes sense to place your identity in Him. Mold yourself after the Creator, not the created.

Another way to identify idols in your life is to consider the things or people that pull you away from God rather than bring you closer to Him. School was the thing that pulled me further away from God. For a long time, I preferred to study and complete assignments than spend time with God. I felt that studying or doing schoolwork would produce a better reward than spending time with God.

I am not saying that going to school and being a good student is bad. I am just pointing out that our lives must be balanced and appropriately prioritized. If you are a student, you should not be so consumed by your workload that you do not have time to sit at the feet of God.

Also, integrating God into your academic life is far better than excluding Him. Once I started putting God first by praying, worshipping, and studying the Bible before tackling assignments for school, I felt less anxious. I was more at peace because I trusted God to help me excel in school instead of solely relying on myself. The Lord truly came through for me!

Idols can also be things you feel you cannot live without. Many people feel that they cannot live without their significant other or certain family members. They prioritize these people in their lives. Sometimes, in their quest to not lose these people, they put them above God.

By choosing to please anyone you feel you cannot live without over God, you make an idol out of them. People make terrible gods. They cannot fill the God-sized voids in your life. They cannot love you better than God, your Creator, can.

Idols may be the thing that is consuming most of your time and thoughts as well. Social media can be an idol in your life if you are on social media so much that you do not have much time to do anything else. Some people spend numerous hours scrolling through social media, so they lack physical and social interaction or are not doing anything to improve their skillset. Even when they are away from social media for a while, their thoughts are consumed with it.

Of course, social media can have great benefits. However, it should not consume all your time. People addicted to social media do not have much time to spend with God. They can pick up a spirit of comparison or whatever spirit they follow on their social media accounts. Since they are not spending time with God, they may not realize that they have picked up these spirits, so they cannot cast them out.

Another tool that can help you identify idols in your life is to think of the people whose opinions you value more than anything. Many people idolize celebrities. They spend a lot of time stalking them on social media. They want to know everything they possibly can about their favorite celebrities. They copy a lot of things that they see these celebrities do and sometimes even adopt their ideologies.

Matthew 6:24 says, *"No one can serve two masters; for either he will hate the one and love the other, or else he will be loyal to the one and despise the other. You cannot serve God and mammon."* The problem with serving God while having idols is that you cannot be loyal to both. You will end up compromising something.

If you lose your loyalty and devotion to God to sustain an idol, your purity will be impacted. Celebrities are human beings. They are not perfect. Even if most of their actions are positive, they can lead you astray because they are not perfect.

However, Christ is perfect, and He will never fail you. All of God's ways are intentional. He intentionally does things to prosper you and not fail you. He wants you to be successful and have an abundant life.

Sometimes, we have idols in our lives because we do not fully trust in God. I idolized getting good grades because I wanted to have a successful future. If I genuinely believed that God had a great plan to prosper me, I would not had put so much pressure on myself to obtain good grades. I would have been significantly less anxious knowing that God was in control.

When I got to the point where all I wanted to do was please God and follow His will for my life, I didn't put so much pressure on myself to pass my classes and graduate. I just put my faith in God and trusted that He would help me accomplish everything I needed.

Romans 1:24-25 (MSG) says, "*...It wasn't long before they were living in a pigpen, smeared with filth, filthy inside and out. And all this because they traded the true God for a fake god and worshipped the god they made instead of the God who made them – the God we bless, the God who blesses us.*"

These verses prove that there are consequences for having idols. People who worship false gods do not live their best lives. The people Paul is talking about had an inferior life because they preferred to worship a fake god rather than the true living God. We miss out on specific blessings when we have idols in our lives.

I pray that you become aware of any idols you may have in your life. I pray that you garner the strength to get rid of any idols that are affecting your relationship with God. I pray that Christ becomes enough for you and you become whole in Him. May the Holy Spirit grant you wisdom and discernment as you prioritize your life so Christ can be first.

Chapter 5:

Obtaining Purity Through the Word of God

A major aspect of obtaining purity is studying the Word of God. Psalm 119:9 says, "*How can a young man keep his way pure? By guarding it according to your word.*" When we read the Bible, we feed our spirit with positive, pure information. By doing this, our perception is purified, and we become individuals who walk in true purity.

A lot of people misjudge scripture and view it as boring because they are not reading it most beneficially. Psalm 119:105 says, "*By your words, I can see where I'm going; they throw a beam of light on my dark path.*" The Bible gives us the knowledge to navigate through life. If you are struggling to find life direction from the Word of God, I implore you to engage the Holy Spirit as you read the scriptures.

The Bible is so much more meaningful when it is read with the help of the Holy Spirit. The Holy Spirit should be your guide as you study the scripture, revealing how the scripture applies to your life. The instances where I prayed for the Holy Spirit's help when studying the Word were far more exciting and life-changing than times when I just opened my Bible and read what I felt like reading.

When studying the Bible, ask the Holy Spirit to guide your interpretation of the scriptures so you can gain what God wants you to gain. Another best practice in Bible study is to read a scripture that applies to what is occurring in your life. For instance, if you are struggling with sexual purity, you should be reading scripture about sexual purity.

One particular scripture that gives us an action to take concerning sex is First Corinthians 6:18-20. The NLT version of these verses states, *"Run from sexual sin! No other sin so clearly affects the body as this one does. For sexual immorality is a sin against one's own body. Don't you realize that your body is the temple of the Holy Spirit, who lives in you and was given to you by God? You do not belong to yourself, for God bought you at a high price. So you must honor God with your body."*

These verses provide a lot of information. The first main point is that there are sexual practices that God considers sinful. The second important thing these verses point out is that sexual sin affects you in different ways than other types of sin. Finally, these verses show that as a Christian, your body is a temple that belongs to God, and you should honor God with your body by obeying Him.

Colossians 3:5 is another verse that talks about sex in the Bible. The NKJV version of this verse is, *"Therefore put to death your members which are on the earth: fornication, uncleanness, passion, evil desire, and covetousness, which is idolatry."*

In this verse, God is calling us to kill fornication. He doesn't say to pause it for a while or that it is acceptable to do it if you're really in love. When something is put to death, it is gone forever. Colossians 3:5 makes it clear that God does not want us to engage in sex outside of marriage at all. I love how Proverbs 5:15-17 talks about sex. The NLT version of these verses states, *"Drink water from your own well—share your love only with your wife. Why spill the water of your springs in the streets, having sex with just anyone? You should reserve it for yourselves. Never share it with strangers."*

Proverbs 5:15-17 reveal how beautiful and sacred sex should be regarded. It is a practice that should be reserved for marriage only. This sacred act should not happen with just any random person you meet on the street, in the club, at your place of employment, in a store, or even in church. Sex should occur between two people who are truly committed to each other through marriage.

I gave three examples of scriptures that talk about sex in the Bible. More references to sex in the Bible can be found in Revelation 2:20, Galatians 5:19–21, 1 Thessalonians 4:3-5, Hebrews 13:4, 1Corinthians 6:13, Ephesians 5:3, Ephesians 5:5, and 2 Corinthians 12:21. I implore you to read these verses and write down the revelation God provides through them.

If you are not very familiar with the Bible and do not know which scriptures relate to a situation that you are facing, there are a few things that you can do. You can pray and ask God to show you which scriptures to study. If you feel that God did not give you an answer after praying, then you can search for keywords in the back of your Bible in the concordance section. You can also search for scriptures on Google.

Simply type,

"Scripture about__________________________________."

(Insert area that you need Godly wisdom in)

You can search for scriptures about anything, for example, purity, finances, relationships, etc. God's word has so many jewels for successful living.

I intentionally mentioned praying to God first because He knows the perfect scriptures that you need to study in a particular season. There have been times when God led me to scriptures that I thought did not apply to my situation, but they ended up being exactly what I needed. The Bible is God's beautiful love letter to you. Read it with the joy and excitement it is meant to be read with.

Bible study becomes mundane and legalistic without the assistance of the Holy Spirit. Hebrews 4:12 says, "For the word of

God is alive and powerful. It is sharper than the sharpest two-edged sword, cutting between soul and spirit, between joint and marrow. It exposes our innermost thoughts and desires." I am a living witness that God's word exposes our inner thoughts and desires. I learned things about myself that I did not know when reading God's Word. It is truly amazing.

I mentioned that studying scriptures applicable to situations you are dealing with helps make the scripture more interesting and personal. However, it is essential to read all scripture. Second Timothy 3:16-17 (NIV) says, *"All Scripture is God-breathed and is useful for teaching, rebuking, correcting, and training in righteousness, so that the servant of God may be thoroughly equipped for every good work."* This verse intentionally uses the word "ALL" to describe which scriptures are useful, not some, so we should spend time studying ALL of them, not only the popular ones or the ones we think we could relate to the most.

I pray that your relationship with God grows tremendously as you diligently seek Him by reading His word. I pray that you gain purity in every contaminated area of your life. May the Holy Spirit lead and guide you as you study the scriptures so that your life can be permanently transformed. May God bring you great pleasure and joy as you are washed with His word.

Chapter 6:

Pure Praise

Another key component of living a pure life is praise. Philippians 1:10-11 says, "*...and so be pure and blameless for the day of Christ, being filled with the fruit of righteousness that comes through Jesus Christ, to the glory and praise of God.*" This verse proves that we praise God when we are pure, blameless, and made righteous through Christ.

Many people limit praise to singing a Christian song or hymn. People may also limit praise to shouting or saying words of adoration to God. Singing songs or verbally expressing our admiration for God are great ways to express our praise to God. However, they are not the only ways we can praise Him.

The Cambridge Dictionary defines praise as "to honor, worship, and express admiration for a god." We can honor Him with more than just our words. We can honor Him with our entire lives and bodies.

I love The Message version of Romans 12:1. It says, "*God helping you: Take your everyday, ordinary life—your sleeping, eating, going-to-work, and walking-around life—and place it before God as an offering. Embracing what God does for you is the best thing you can do for him.*"

When we walk in obedience to what God has called us to do, we honor Him; therefore, we praise Him. We can praise God through our daily activities as well. When you are kind and respectful to others, you are honoring God.

When you take care of the things God has blessed you with, like your car, living accommodations, and clothes, you are honoring God. When you abstain from premarital sex, you honor God with your body and praise Him. When practicing the fruit of the spirit, you bring honor to God's name.

In Colossians 3:23, we are encouraged to *"work willingly at whatever [we] do, as though [we] were working for the Lord rather than for people."* This is yet another instruction from the Bible that encourages us to keep God in mind with everything we do. Sometimes, we get mad at our boss or a customer and decide not to go the extra mile for them. However, the Bible tells us not to work as if we were working solely for that boss or customer who upset us.

We should work as if we were working for the one true living God. If your customer or boss upsets you, move beyond that. Think about serving God while working and still giving it your all. This is also useful to prevent us from making idols out of achieving worldly success. Instead of ignoring God and working solely for earthly gain, you are putting God first by focusing on working to please Him.

When we honor God through our daily actions, we praise Him. Remember Philippians 1:10-11; when our actions are pure, then we are praising God through our actions. When we are pure in how we treat people, God is glorified and praised through our actions.

The best way we can praise God is with our hearts; then, the actions and words of adoration will follow. God makes it clear in His word that we cannot truly honor Him with our words and actions if we do not honor Him with our hearts. If we do not honor Him in our hearts, then our words and actions of praise are not pure.

In Isaiah 29:13, God says, *"These people make a big show of saying the right thing, but their hearts aren't in it. Because they act like they're worshipping me but don't mean it."* It does not please God when we pretend to worship Him with our hearts and actions, but our hearts are far from Him. He knows that this kind of worship is not sincere.

Sometimes, people make a big show out of praising God with their mouths because they believe it will bring them some sort of earthly reward. They think they will get promoted to a leadership position at church if their praise is extravagant. Or sometimes, people try to impress someone that they are attracted to with their praise. They think they can win over their affection with praise that looks deep. This proves that they care more about the affections of man than God.

Wouldn't you be offended if someone bought you a nice gift just to show off in front of others? When the two of you are alone, they ignore you, but when other people are around, they show their love and affection for you.

They may post pictures of you two on social media with favorable captions to get a lot of likes. However, they do not genuinely care about you. I am confident you would not want to be in a relationship with someone like that. Nobody wants to be used. So why treat God that way?

Do a self-check. Reflect on whether you truly love God. How do you show love to God? Think about which things may distract you or impede you from honoring God with your heart. What do you care more about than pleasing God? What are you filling your heart with so God does not have space to enter?

Ask God to forgive you if you have not been praising from a pure heart. Ask Him to "*Create in [you] a clean heart... [and] renew a right spirit within [you]*" (Psalms 51:10). Trust that He will fill your heart and make it pure. Follow the leading of the Holy Spirit as He directs you on how to keep your heart pure.

God does not need our worship. Do not think that you are doing God a favor by praising Him. Doing this cheapens the praise and worship experience. In Luke 19:40, Jesus says, *"...if these should keep silent, the stones would immediately cry out."*

God is the Creator of the entire universe and everything in it. If He needed worship, He could have anything worship Him. The word "immediately" in Luke 19:40 shows how powerful God is. He does not need to take time to gather the stones and complete some sort of long methodology to make the stones worship. The stones would cry out in an instant.

It is a privilege to praise God, and we should adopt this attitude when doing so. It is an honor and privilege to have the opportunity to praise the Creator of the universe. Communicating with God and expressing love, adoration, and appreciation to Him is a blessing.

When we praise God, we invite His presence. Psalm 22:3 says, *"But thou art holy, O thou that inhabitest the praises of Israel."* This verse means that God dwells where His praises are. If you are distant from God or want to feel closer to His presence, I implore you to bridge the gap between you and Him with praise.

God's presence comes with an abundance of blessings. Psalm 16:11 says, *"In your presence is fullness of joy; at your right hand are pleasure forevermore."* When we praise God from a pure heart, we become joyful because God is present. The next time you are feeling down and upset, praise God.

I pray that you have many encounters with God as you praise Him from a pure heart. May your praise grant you access to the joy and peace of God. I pray that you praise the Lord with a heart of gratitude and admiration. You will notice that you feel more joyful and at peace the more you praise God.

Chapter 7:

Pure Identity/Self-Worth

For a long time, I thought I had high self-worth. I was confident in the fact that I was beautiful, smart, and pleasant. It was easy to make friends because people generally liked me. I received a lot of attention from males who were physically attracted to me.

Well, I discovered holes in my self-confidence when I went to university. I was a woman of color at a predominantly white institution (P.W.I.) in the United States. While I loved the university I attended, I encountered some challenges. There were significant differences between my university life and the life I was accustomed to in The Bahamas, and this affected my self-worth.

Firstly, there were not a lot of men who were interested in me or even checking me out. Everyone also knew that I was a Christian, so there were not many men approaching me for a casual date or "Netflix and Chill." For the first time in my life, I could not depend on other people to validate my beauty.

My university experience caused me to lose some self-confidence in my physical appearance. It also made me feel less valuable as a person holistically. There were many instances where my friends of color and I felt invisible. People walked into us or did not acknowledge our presence when they entered a room we were in.

Sometimes, our contributions to group projects seem not to be heard or valued. I remember being the only person of color in many of my classes. That feeling alone is not so great. It is on a whole other level when you are treated like you are different or do not belong.

I will NEVER forget my very first Spanish class during my first semester of college. I arrived at the class early, and everyone who came in after me sat on the opposite side of the room from where I sat. I felt isolated and inferior. Eventually, one Caucasian female walked in and sat next to me. A few others sat on our side of the classroom after that.

This is how most of my college career was. Some people were not particularly friendly to me. Some people talked to me in class but pretended they did not know me outside class. Do not get me wrong, I had friends, so I was not lonely. My self-confidence suffered some damage because several people rejected me instead of being warm to me like I was accustomed to.

Not only did I feel less valuable physically and socially, I doubted whether I was smart. I worked hard and got great grades throughout my school career. However, when I went to college, my grades were mediocre. No matter how hard I worked, how much I studied, or how many times I went to a professor's office hours, I never got the high grades that I desperately desired.

There were some classes that I did well in, but they felt few and far between. I knew that my self-confidence was diminishing, but I did not realize the deeper impact of my university career until I was journaling one day. I journal as a means to pour my heart out to God intentionally. I talk to God a lot throughout the day, but I find that when I journal, I tap into depths of my heart and emotions that I never knew existed. I am truly bare before the Lord.

After journaling one day and pouring out about those disappointing moments, God told me why He allowed me to go through everything I did in college. Yes! I know it sounds absurd, but God ALLOWED me to have those negative experiences! Lamentations 3:37-38 says, *"Who can command things to happen without the Lord's permission? Does not the Most High send both calamity and good?"* The Bible proves that God allows both good and bad things to happen to us. However, the bad things are not necessarily to punish us. God often allows difficult things to happen because He is pruning us. John 15:2 says, *"Every branch in me that does not bear fruit He takes away; and every branch that bears fruit He prunes, that it may bear more fruit."*

The Oxford Dictionary defines prune as "trim (a tree, shrub, or bush) by cutting away dead or overgrown branches or stems, especially to encourage growth." When God prunes us, He rids us of our negative behaviors and patterns so we can grow. He does this because He sees potential in us. Pruning is an incredibly good thing.

Pruning can feel hard because it is difficult to break habits, stop doing things you enjoy, or end certain relationships, but the result is very rewarding. Sometimes the things we stop doing and relationships that end negatively impact our identity and self-worth. Although it may feel painful, it can be rewarding to end these things so our identity and self-worth can be purified.

It is an honor to be pruned by God. Instead of complaining about it or avoiding it, push through the process with a grateful heart. You will be a better person when it is done, and you will be able to serve the kingdom of God in a greater capacity.

God provides consolation in Romans 8:28, which informs us that "God causes everything to work together for the good of those who love God and are called according to His purpose for them." I love the word "everything" in this scripture verse. Some people believe that God cannot use their embarrassing moments or the lowest moments in their lives, but the Bible tells us that God can use ALL of them and cause them to work together for our good.

I urge you to sit before God and ask Him to show you how He can work in your worst situations for good. Sometimes He has already used that situation to benefit you, but you have not noticed it yet. God informed me that He used those disappointing moments during my college career to rid me of my dependence on the world for validation.

God could have blessed me with everything I needed to be socially and academically successful in college; however, He did not because He preferred for me to be successful in life. He knew of the great plans that He had for my life.

He knew that I would crumble under pressure if my validation only came from the world. Then humans would still have the special power to crush me, and I would do things that pleased man instead of God.

This taught me that God cares more about our true success in life than our feelings. He doesn't always give us the things that would bring us temporary, instant satisfaction. At the right time, God provides the tools that would allow us to have true success.

Desiring validation from humans derailed my purification process a bit because it distracted me from focusing on what truly mattered, pleasing God. Instead of thinking of ways to please God, I thought of how I could get the approval of others. I was thinking more about what the world deemed successful than God's definition of success.

Before attending university, my identity was in the world. Man confirmed favorable attributes to me, like my beauty, intelligence, and popularity. However, God wanted my identity to be in Him. I am valuable because God created me. I have worth because I am an heiress, a child of the King of Kings. First Peter 2:9-10 says, *"But you are the ones chosen by God, chosen by the high calling of priestly work, chosen to be a holy people, God's instruments to do his work and speak out for him, to tell others the night and day difference he made for you – from nothing to something, from rejected to accepted."*

You are chosen! That means God has options, but He sees something great and unique about you, so He selected you over others. You are God's chosen! Get that in your mind and spirit. He selected you, He called you, He preferred you. Why care about what mere humans think when the ultimate being in the universe favors you?

I want to encourage you to take a moment and reflect on what your identity is currently found in. I am not saying that feeling good when you receive a compliment is bad. It is normal for humans to feel good when someone compliments them. It is dangerous when you depend on those compliments to feel good about yourself.

Some people validate themselves. During my college days, I had to believe that I was beautiful even though nobody confirmed this. I validated myself. Sometimes, I would look in the mirror before going out and tell myself that I was beautiful.

Different cultures have different measures of value because of how they have been conditioned and trained. Where you grew up influences how you see yourself, what you appreciate about yourself, what you notice about yourself, and how you value yourself. I had to learn to find my identity in Christ ultimately. I realized that I was fearfully and wonderfully made for a purpose.

There is something that will always influence the way you see yourself. I pray that you decide to make God your main influence.

Ephesians 2:10 says, *"For we are God's masterpiece. He has created us anew in Christ Jesus, so we can do the good things he planned for us long ago."* Isn't that amazing? The Creator of the universe considers you to be His masterpiece. Remember that you are God's masterpiece whenever you are feeling down or have a moment where your confidence is weak. God created you to fulfill the plans He made for your life long ago.

What is influencing how you view yourself? God or the world? Would you still feel valuable if nobody gave you another compliment for the rest of your life? If nobody affirmed that thing God told you to do, would you still feel like you did something great because you were obedient to God?

There is a special freedom in having pure self-worth. I pray that you fully experience this. I pray that God restores the years and emotions that were wasted while you searched for value and identity in the wrong places.

May you realize and genuinely believe just how special you are to God. You may have been rejected by your family, peers, co-workers, fellow church members, etc., but God did not reject you. Your life carries great value and meaning. May God's peace and assurance dwell with you always. Selah (If this prayer touched you, I implore you to write it down and place it in a special place where you will be reminded of it.)

Chapter 8:

Purity vs. Abstinence

There is a great difference between sexual purity and abstaining from sex. People who practice sexual purity abstain from sex before marriage; however, everyone who abstains from sex is not practicing sexual purity. People decide not to be abstinent for many different reasons. Many people decide to abstain because people with whom they had sexual relations in the past mistreated them. They want to wait until they heal or until they meet someone who makes them feel secure. However, true security can only be found in God.

One of the main reasons I decided to wait until marriage when I was younger was the fear of getting pregnant at a young age. I grew up seeing people who got pregnant at a young age and were not married.

I could tell that life became more difficult for them after having children, and I did not want to endure the same hardships. I do not look down on unmarried people who get pregnant at a young age. After seeing those who did, I understood that their lives were more complex due to this. I was fully aware of the birth control options available; however, I did not want to take the chance.

After some self-assessment and growth in my relationship with God, I realized that my fear of becoming pregnant should not be higher than my desire to honor God with my life and body. God took me on a journey where He showed me that He wants people to remain sexually pure, and He gave me wisdom on how I can remain a virgin until marriage.

In Second Timothy 2:22, we are encouraged to *"Flee also youthful lusts, but pursue righteousness, faith, love, and peace with those who call on the Lord out of a pure heart."* Purity is a heart issue. This is what differentiates people who are sexually pure from sexually abstinent people.

Sexually abstinent people are abstaining from having sex but are not necessarily abstaining from everything that compromises their purity.

Sexually pure people abstain from physically having sex and are trying to live a lifestyle where they have pure thoughts and are not compromising their purity.

The sexually pure abstain from sex because they want to honor God with their lives. They are not just abstaining from sex, but abstaining from any sexual thoughts or actions that are not pleasing to God.

Some sexually abstinent people are abstaining for selfish reasons. They have pure actions that are not the result of a pure heart. Their hearts are not absolutely free from adulteration or contamination. Some still entertain impure thoughts or activities. They go as far as they can without technically engaging in sex.

Some even lust after people in their minds and do not cast down these thoughts. This is not a pure thing to do. Matthew 5:28-29 warns against lustful thoughts by saying, *"...anyone who even looks at a woman with lust has already committed adultery with her in his heart. So if your eye—even your good eye causes you to lust, gouge it out and throw it away. It is better for you to lose one part of your body than for your whole body to be thrown into hell."*

This scripture makes it plain that God regards lustful thoughts seriously. Gouging your eye out is very extreme. God wants us to go to extreme measures to obtain purity.

For instance, extreme measures could be taken when traveling with your significant other before marriage. You can either buy two separate hotel rooms or travel with a group of people who support your sexual purity journey. You can even decide not to take any trips with your boyfriend, girlfriend, or fiancé until you are married.

When impure thoughts creep into our minds, we should cast them down. God is not satisfied with pure fruit solely; He wants us to have pure fruit (pure actions) and pure roots (pure heart and mind).

The story of Jephthah and his daughter in Judges 11 gives a good example of someone with a pure heart. To summarize, Jephthah is the son of a promiscuous woman. He made a promise to give God whatever comes out of the door of his house to meet him when he returns from battle if God gives him a clean victory over the Ammonites. Jephthah's only child, his virgin daughter, was the first to come out of his house to greet him.

Jephthah's heart was torn to shreds, but he kept his vow to the Lord. Jephthah's daughter only asked her father to give her two months to wander through the hills and lament her virginity since she would never marry. Her father approved, and her friends went with her to lament.

This story has taught me and inspired me in many ways. Firstly, it was encouraging to see how God can completely change any situation. The granddaughter of a promiscuous woman died a virgin. God can restore any situation. There are no limits to what God can do. Luke 1:37 says, *"For with God nothing will be impossible."*

I also admire Jephthah's pure, honest, and committed heart. After he realized his only child would have to be sacrificed. He could have decided not to fulfill his vow to God. Especially since he was so distressed, but he died to his flesh and fulfilled his vow to God. I am certain that this was a traumatic experience for him.

Thirdly, I was also impressed with the purity of Jephthah's daughter's heart. She knew she would die a virgin and did not have much time left on earth. She could have decided to sleep around with different men before she died, but she did not. Being sexually pure was about honoring God and her family. This is truly admirable.

As I think about my admiration for the story of Jephthah and his daughter and how I relate to this. I want to ask you a few questions. I hope that you truly take this moment to reflect on and digest this next section. There is no rush. Be honest with God and with yourself.

If you knew that you would die very soon before you had an opportunity to get married, would you remain faithful to God in the area of your sexual purity? What is the purpose of your sexual purity? Are you pursuing your sexually pure lifestyle solely because you want to marry the right person? Or are you sexually pure so you can worship God with your obedience?

Psalm 51:10 says, *"Make me loyal to you, Lord! Please make me loyal to your vision, purpose, and will for my life."* The psalmist, David, realized that he would need the help of the Lord if he wanted to become loyal to the Lord. It does not make sense to pretend with God. He knows everything anyway. We grow closer to God and receive deliverance when we are completely honest with Him.

Where does your loyalty lie? If your loyalty does not honestly lie with God, then pray Psalm 51:10 over your life. Even if you are already loyal to God, you should pray this verse over your life as a form of reinforcement. Sometimes our loyalty needs to be strengthened, or we need to enter a deeper level of loyalty to the Lord.

The more loyal you are to God, you will notice that your desires align more with His desires for your life. This will help to give you longevity and success in your Christian journey.

Desiring after the wrong things can distract you and weaken your relationship with God. Your desires will match your heart posture. If your heart takes joy and pleasure in worldly things like fame and fortune, you will desire that. However, if you take joy and pleasure in God, then you will desire the fruit of the spirit and things of the Lord. Your loyalty to God would be strong.

I pray that God grants you strength and endurance on your sexual purity journey. I pray that you understand and adapt to the right reasons for practicing abstinence. If you are currently struggling, I pray that you have a change of heart and motives after reading and reflecting. May not only your physical actions have the appearance of purity, but may your heart posture be pure as well.

Chapter 9:

The Inconvenience of Sexual Purity (Some Reasons Why People Decide Not to Wait)

We live in a fast-paced, instant society. People are making decisions quickly without giving them much thought. This is because they are afraid that the opportunity will not exist for a long time or do not have much patience. I have also noticed that a lot of companies are now using this as a marketing strategy. They have sales for a small window of time, so we are forced to make a quick decision that is not properly thought out. I have fallen into this trap of buying on impulse a few times, but I am learning to use more wisdom with my spending.

Some people take this same impulse mentality into other areas of their lives, like their sex life. They are attracted to someone, and their hormones are flowing, so after a date or two... or no dates at all (let's be real), they decide to have sex with that person. It was not a very well-thought-out decision and might be regretted later on.

The desire to have sex is completely understandable and expected. One of the reasons God created us is for reproduction. To reproduce, we must have sexual desires. It is normal to desire sex but being a slave or having no restraints on your sexual desires should not be normal.

"Be true to yourself" is a very popular phrase that makes people feel powerful and liberated. However, we need to think about this statement and explore the fullness of what it means. People love to use this statement to condone their sins. Although they know what they are doing is a sin, and it displeases God, they take pride in doing it because they are being "true to themselves."

A lot of people are even mad at God because they have natural desires that God tells them not to act on. They are conflicted. They believe in God, want to be Christians, and experience His goodness and power; however, obedience to God requires sacrifice. They would have to die to their flesh, which would mean not being true to themselves.

A person controlled by their sexual desires or heavily involved with sex could be faced with the decision to die to themselves and take up Christ's ways. This may be extremely difficult for them. They could argue that they enjoy sex and have no shame in being sexually active outside of marriage, so they are true to themselves.

However, they are living THEIR life by continuing to be true to themselves and engaging in premarital sex. Not the life that Christ has planned for them. They are not yet at the point where they want to do things God's way. They have not totally surrendered their lives to God.

We need to be careful about what we are promoting when we decide to adopt these phrases that make us feel justified and empowered. Would the world truly be better if everyone stayed true to themselves? Or would the world be much better off if people practiced letting their flesh die?

I know dying to your flesh is challenging because you are killing your flesh desires, but it is worth it. It would make you a better person and make the world a better place to live in.

Being selfless is one way that people can die to themselves. One simple example of this can be seen with lying or covering up the truth about something. A person could lie about having an STD or STI because they are embarrassed about it and know there is a good chance that they could be rejected by the person they desire to engage in sexual activities with if they are aware of the STD or STI.

That one lie or omission of vital information could cause the STD or STI to spread to another person, and that person can spread it to someone else. The spread of this STD or STI could have been prevented by the person dying to their flesh and deciding to come clean about their situation. This is just one example of how killing your fleshly desires and being transparent can help the world in a significant way by reducing the spread of STDs and STIs.

Being true to yourself in the area of sex can have a lot of negative consequences. If a married person decides to be true to the sexual desires that they have for someone to whom they are not married, the consequences would be highly unfavorable.

Even single people who decide to engage in pre-marital sex because they want to be true to their sexual desires can end up dealing with severe consequences. A few moments of pleasure can lead to STDs, STIs, heartbreak, confusion, low self-esteem, soul ties, and unplanned pregnancies. It is much more beneficial to die to your flesh than to your relationship with God.

Please do not be mad at God for requiring you to have a disciplined lifestyle. He just wants the best for you. Isaiah 55:9 (NKJV) says, *"For as the heavens are higher than the earth, So are my ways higher than your ways, And my thoughts higher than your thoughts."*

God's approach to life is so much better than yours. You may think it is a good idea to follow your heart and your fleshly desires, but they cannot cause you to live the quality of life that God has for you. Following God's ways will give you a more prosperous and meaningful life.

Instead of being true to your sexual desires, submit them to God through prayer. Matthew 16:24-26 says, *"Then Jesus went to work on His disciples. 'Anyone who intends to come with me has to let me lead. You are not in the driver's seat; I am. Do not run from suffering; embrace it. Follow me, and I'll show you how. Self-help is no help at all. Self-sacrifice is the way, my way, to finding yourself, your true self. What kind of a deal is it to get everything you want but lose yourself? What could you ever trade your soul for?'"*

We must surrender every aspect of our lives to Christ and allow Him to lead, especially our sexual lives. This book sheds some insight into God's desire for our sex lives. However, I urge you to continue exploring this topic by communicating with God more personally. You will have more confidence and determination to be sexually pure once you know God's desire for your sex life.

Sexual temptation is one of the things Jesus talks about when He mentions that we would have to suffer if we wanted to be one of His followers. By dying to our flesh in this area, we develop self-discipline, which is an excellent tool to have in our relationships with others. Oftentimes, we lose ourselves in our effort to obtain quick gratification.

To reiterate, Matthew 16:24-26 mentions, *"Self-sacrifice is the way, my way to finding yourself,* ***your true self****."* When we decide to be sexually pure, we sacrifice our desires. By doing this, we are identifying with our true characteristic of being pure. Our identity is not in the world; it is in Christ. Christ sets the standard for our lives. Christ allows us to find our true selves.

The world has tricked us into thinking being true to ourselves involves following our fleshly desires, but it is quite the opposite for Christians. When you become saved, you are born again. Although it is a process, God gives you His desires. Your true self emulates Christ.

Sometimes we miss out on the opportunity to develop into the people God created. We gain the world's perspective instead of

God's; in doing this, we lose our true selves. The world is constantly bombarding us with their standards for sex in movies, television shows, and songs where pre-marital sex is glorified.

Our true self is the person who God truly created us to be, which is set apart and different from the world. We have to fill ourselves up with the Word of God so we are constantly reminded of the standards God has set for us.

I mentioned one reason why people decide to have sex outside of marriage; their desires or physical needs. Another reason people do not practice abstinence is that they feel like they have to practice to develop great sex skills to please the person they want to be with for the rest of their lives. This is a popular opinion believed by many.

Public opinions are not always true. Just because many believe something is true does not necessarily mean it is true. Do the necessary work to formulate your own opinion about something before blindly accepting the masses' ideology. Many believe that sexual experience outside of marriage makes you a better sex partner, but that is not necessarily true.

It is rare to perfect something the first time you do it. A part of the marriage journey involves learning your spouse's various preferences, and that includes sexual preferences. I have never been married, but I have heard married couples say that sex with their spouse improves over time as they learn their partner's sexual preferences and vice versa. This proves that enhancing communication skills is far more important than enhancing sex skills before marriage. Communication makes sex better.

Also, by having "sex practice" with someone who will not be your future spouse, you may learn sexual habits that your future spouse may not like. If an orthodontist made a retainer for you, they wouldn't use molds from different people's mouths that they had been practicing on to make your retainer. That would be ridiculous because the retainer would fit the person it was modeled with but not you.

This is what happens when you have sex practice with other people before you are sexually intimate with your spouse. You are molded into being a good sexual partner for someone else, not necessarily your spouse. This can leave you with sexual behavior that you have to unlearn. Psychological studies have proven that it is harder to unlearn information than it is to learn something new.

Having sex practice outside of marriage can also cause you to fall into the dilemma of comparing your spouse to your past sexual partners. This can cheapen the sexual experience and even cause you to feel sexually unfulfilled if you still have the desire to be intimate with one of your past sexual partners. This may even result in your spouse feeling rejected.

Sex practice before marriage can also have memories stored in your mind from past sexual encounters. While you are being sexually intimate with your spouse, you may have flashbacks from your former partner replaying in your mind. I believe developing strong communication and trust with your significant other during the dating/courtship and engagement season is essential. This enables you to have honest discussions about sexual preferences or anything else when you are married.

People also choose to engage in premarital sex to see if they are sexually compatible with the person they are interested in before committing. They have taken the car dealership mentality into their romantic lives. They want to test drive the vehicle before they make a purchase.

Sex is just one aspect of the greater overall scheme of things when it comes to marriage. Even if a couple is experiencing sexual dissatisfaction, that does not mean they are being punished or are not "meant to be." Several things can be done to achieve sexual satisfaction once a couple is willing to put the work in to try them.

I do not believe that God will ask you to abstain from sex until marriage and then punish you with a partner who makes you miserable while having sex with them. Matthew 7:11 says, "*If you then, being evil, know how to give good gifts to your children, how much more will your Father who is in heaven give good things to those who ask Him!*" God knows what you like. He created you.

Be prayerful when choosing a future spouse. Get God's approval before marriage. He will bless you with a partner who is fully equipped to walk through life with you now and decades from now. Often, people marry whom they want to marry without consulting God. Then, when they realize they married the wrong person, they become bitter and angry at God because they know God is a proponent of marriage.

Sometimes, people regret getting married and sow bitter seeds about marriage to other people. They tell people to make sure they live with their significant other before they get married to get to know them better before they fully commit. They may even tell people horror stories from their marriage to convince others not to get married.

Not everyone is indeed called to the ministry of marriage, but that is because of how God created them. The Message translation of First Corinthians 7:7-9 says, "*... But abstinence is not for everyone any more than marriage is. God gives the gift of single life to some and the gift of married life to others...*" But if they can't manage their desires and emotions, they should, by all means, go ahead and get married. The difficulties of marriage are preferable by far to a sexually tortured life as a single.

The decision to remain single for the rest of your life should not be motivated by the fear of having a miserable life once you're married. Therefore, it is important to have a relationship with God where you spend time with Him and learn His desires for your life. Your relationship status should be rooted in Christ, not people's opinions.

Another reason people choose to engage in sex outside of marriage is to accommodate their significant other. Sometimes people engage in premarital sex because their significant other is not interested in being sexually abstinent. They have the mindset that if the person they are in a relationship with is not having sex with them, they are getting their needs met with someone else.

Since they do not want that person to cheat on them or break up with them, they give in and engage in sex outside of marriage. By doing this, they are honoring their significant other over God. They are proving that they care more about pleasing the person they are in a relationship with than God. Their significant other is their idol.

Sexual sin can be rooted in misplaced priorities. Instead of prioritizing your relationship with God, you prioritize your relationship with your partner. This is evident when sex is involved. However, it can also be seen in other ways. Some people are so consumed with their significant other that they do not have time to spend with God. This is also evidence of misplaced priorities.

To further expound upon my previous point, I would like to note that if your relationship ends because you've decided not to have sex with your significant other, this could mean that this is not the right person for you in this season or totality. If you are in this situation, I want to encourage you to seek God's guidance on whether this person is not suitable for you in totality or whether they are not the right fit for this season of your life.

You and your significant other should be equally yoked, which means they should share your spiritual beliefs and convictions. Anyone who draws you away from God instead of encouraging you to walk in the ways of Christ and pushing you closer to Christ may be sent from the enemy and not God. One excellent way to spot a counterfeit is to consider whether it brings you closer to God or causes you to drift further away. Do not be afraid to get rid of counterfeits.

Your sexuality is far more important than establishing a relationship with a man or woman. God values our sexuality so much more than that; we should too. I would like to reiterate Matthew 16:25 in the New International Version. This verse says, "*... whoever wants to save their life will lose it, but whoever loses their life for me will find it.*" You may try to save your "romantic life" by having sex. However, if you give up having sex for God, then He can bless you with an even better romantic life. This can help you to have a better life overall.

When God removes someone from our lives, He always brings someone or something better. Sometimes that better thing is healing, peace, or new self-confidence. You may go through a process before meeting the person that God has for you to be with.

Take time to mourn the relationship but be encouraged by the fact that God will bring you someone who is better suited for you. Many people waste years with the wrong person because they have developed a soul tie or do not think God will send them someone better. Meanwhile, God is simply waiting for you to let go of the person to make room for the person He has ordained for you to be with.

Some people choose to engage in sex before marriage because they think it is a sign that they are mature. They believe that once they have sex, they will become a real man or woman. They think that while they are still virgins, they have not achieved manhood or womanhood yet.

In some spheres of society, true manhood or womanhood is believed to be attained once virginity is lost. However, there are so many things that go into being a mature adult other than having sex. A mature adult is capable of making sound decisions, being responsible, able to provide for themselves and their family, etc.

When you think about it, children can engage in sexual activity if they want to. There are instances, although fairly uncommon, where children have been caught engaging in sexual activities with each other. Does this mean that they are now adults? Can they go out into the world and fend for themselves now?

Of course not. They are not even old enough to get jobs. Many people have their first sexual experience as teenagers. Teenagers are not fully developed mentally or physically. It would be fallacious for them to think they are grown because they have had sex. (Although many of them think that they are.)

Jesus Christ gives us the perfect example of adulthood. He was the only perfect human to ever live on earth. The Bible teaches us so much about true adulthood through the life of Jesus. The Bible does not mention anything about Jesus having sex and making Him the perfect mature man. That is because sex is not necessary to attain maturity.

Your standard needs to be Christ in every area of your life. That would save you from doing a lot of unnecessary things for the sake of acceptance or false feelings of security. It is amazing how many people pursue accomplishments such as losing their virginity or getting married to prove that they are mature. However, they never pursue real character development.

Many people believe that their bodies are their greatest asset, so they decide to have premarital sex to lure their love interest. They are convinced that the person will be hooked once they reveal their entire attractive body and show off their great sex moves. There are a plethora of songs and movies that portray this mindset and convince people to think along these lines.

This method occasionally works, but when it does, it results in a shallow sex-based relationship. Also, if all it took was sex moves for you to win someone over, then someone else with even better moves could win them away from you. There must be something more significant than sex at the root of a relationship.

Sex has a shallow root system. Plants with shallow roots are easily uprooted and sometimes damage the surrounding environment when they are uprooted. To withstand any storm, your relationship should be firmly and deeply rooted. You should have a relationship where Christ is at the center, keeping you rooted. Show off your God moves instead of your sex moves.

Pre-marital sex can create false hope and bitterness. A superficial relationship based on sex is unfulfilling. You will always feel like something is missing, and that is because A LOT is missing. I know someone who was in a strictly sexual relationship. The only thing they did together was have sex. The female in this relationship thought the male liked her because he continued to have regular sex with her. He did like her, but only for her body.

He was not interested in pursuing anything further. She was not the only person whom he was having sexual relations with at the time, and she knew. However, she still held on to the hope that there could be something more between them. She was heartbroken when she realized there would be nothing more between them. She could have saved herself a huge heartache if she had decided to abstain from sex.

God gave us an example in the Bible of how sex does not necessarily lead to true love. In Genesis 29:32–35, Leah conceived and bore four sons, hoping to win over her husband's affection. The amount of sex they had and the number of children she bore for him did not change his affection toward her. If sex indeed causes someone to fall in love with you, then her husband should have been deeply in love with her after the fourth son.

There is a great difference between someone being in love with your body and someone being in love with you as an individual. If someone is only in love with your body, then the love is very superficial. God forbid, if your body changes or you cannot be physically intimate with them, they will not love you anymore.

However, if the person took the time out to get to know you as an individual and fall in love with who you are holistically, then you would have a much stronger bond. Your love would be able to endure more trials.

The idea that sex is the best thing you can offer someone is usually rooted in low self-esteem. You are far more than just a body to have sex with. Anyone who wants to be with you just for sex should not be with you at all because they are just using you. If you are struggling with self-esteem, I encourage you to pray and ask God to show you what He values about you.

God values you so much that He sent His only son to die on the cross for your sins! Ask God to allow you to see yourself the way He sees you. I encourage you to read Ephesians 1 and 2 to understand your identity in Christ. If your identity is not pure, your lifestyle will not be pure. My prayer is that you develop a pure lifestyle through Jesus Christ and that you reap the benefits of that pure lifestyle.

Chapter 10:

Why wait? The Importance of Sexual Purity

We spent some time discussing why people choose not to be sexually pure. Now let's explore more of what the Bible says about sex outside of marriage. Ephesians 5:3 says, *"But fornication and all uncleanness or covetousness, let it not even be named among you, as is fitting for the saints."* The Bible talks about being sexually pure on different occasions. However, I believe people do not take this commandment seriously because they do not understand the implications of sexual impurity.

It is essential to understand the reason why God wants us to be sexually pure so you can agree with Him and that your season of abstinence is not a big religious act. I firmly believe that if more Christians understood why God wants them to remain sexually pure, then they would not give in to this particular sin. First Corinthians 3:16 says, *"Do you not know that you are the temple of God and that the Spirit of God dwells in you?"* Your body belongs to God. Therefore, you should honor Him in the decisions you make concerning your body. We were created for worship, not dishonor.

God has given us so many different gifts that it would be impossible for us ever to repay Him. He is more than deserving of our love, admiration, and obedience. We should obey God because we want to show Him our love and respect.

John 14:15 says, *"If you love me, obey my commandments."* It is really that simple. You should obey the God that you claim to love so much. Think of someone who you love and respect. Would you intentionally do something that you know that person does not want you to do? No, because you care about them, you try not to intentionally do things that would disappoint them or make them upset.

Sometimes we take God for granted. In His word, He promises never to leave us nor forsake us (Deuteronomy 31:6), so we are not as concerned about pleasing Him as we are about pleasing other people. We know that people tend to remain in our lives or leave based on how we treat them, whereas God is more forgiving, patient, and understanding. Nothing can separate us from the love of God. (Romans 8:38–39).

We should not treat God poorly just because our actions do not affect whether He loves us or not. We should love and honor God even more because He loves us despite everything we do that offends Him. Don't fake it. Be obedient to God because you want to please Him. Do you truly want God to be pleased with your life? Your sexual purity should be a joyful service unto the Lord.

God's word gives more reasons why we should practice sexual purity. The Bible also talks about fornication being a sin against your own body. First Corinthians 6:18 says, "*Flee from sexual immorality. Every other sin a person commits is outside the body, but the sexually immoral person sins against his own body.*" Most people would not intentionally inflict harm on themselves. People tend to avoid being hurt or in pain on any level.

The same diligence people take not to injure themselves with a knife while cooking or avoid accidents while driving should be used to refrain from having sex outside of marriage. When people sin against their bodies, they create unnecessary pain or strife for themselves. The Bible tells us in Romans 6:23 that "*the wages of sin is death.*" When people sin against their bodies, they are pronouncing death upon their bodies.

You must be wondering how this could be since you may have sinned against your own body and know people who have sinned against their bodies, and you are still alive today. There are multiple definitions of "death" in the dictionary. The New Oxford American Dictionary defines death as "the permanent ending of vital processes in a cell or tissue." This is probably what most people think of when the word "death" is mentioned.

However, The New Oxford American Dictionary also defines death as "the destruction or permanent end of something." When you sin against your body, you put an end to some things that were meant for your benefit. The things that die can vary. Some people experience spiritual, financial, and emotional death or death in their self-confidence and identity.

Some people's spiritual lives should be more advanced than they are because they became Christians many years ago. Because of their sexual sin, there is no pulse in their relationship with God. Sexual sin can also cause marriages to die. There have been instances where unfaithful spouses caused distrust in marriage, resulting in divorce.

Romans 6:21 talks about the fruit that leads to death. It says, *"But what fruit were you getting at that time from the things of which you are now ashamed? For the end of those things is death."* One example of a fruit that leads to death is lust. It can lead to the death of healthy relationships and family structures. It can also destroy your health because acting on lustful thoughts can lead to STDs.

Some people have died from illnesses such as AIDS (Acquired Immunodeficiency Syndrome) because they had sex outside of marriage. The continuation of casual sex outside marriage has caused HIV (Human Immunodeficiency Virus) to spread to countless people. Even married people end up contracting HIV from their spouses who are unfaithful to them, resulting in their death if it is untreated.

I have noticed that HIV and AIDS are not talked about as much anymore. There was a time when HIV and AIDS were popular topics on television; however, they are no longer discussed. They did not disappear. People are still spreading HIV, knowingly and unknowingly.

According to the World Health Organization, 1.7 million people became newly infected with HIV in 2018. There were also 770,000 deaths related to HIV in 2018. This proves that although the media may not be talking about it as much, HIV and AIDS are still existent and very dangerous.

If you are sexually active, I implore you to get tested for HIV. People who find out that they have this virus earlier can take treatment for it and live a much longer life than those who do not. Getting tested may seem nerve-wracking and embarrassing, but it is worth it. It is literally a matter of life and death.

It may help to take a friend with you when you get tested. Although I am a virgin, I went with a friend to get tested before because they were nervous about going alone. Although this friend was using contraception, they wanted to be sure that they did not contract anything because contraception is not 100% effective in preventing the spread of STDs.

Romans 6:22 is a contrast to verse 21 as it talks about the fruit that leads to life. It says, "*But now that you have been set free from sin and have become slaves of God, the fruit you get leads to sanctification and its end, eternal life.*" Some examples of good fruit are the fruits of the spirit. Galatians 5:22-23 mentions, "*But the fruit of the Spirit is love, joy, peace, patience, kindness, goodness, faithfulness, gentleness, self-control…*"

I hope you get the idea that sin is so much deeper than you think. God is not trying to make you suffer or require you to accomplish the impossible. It is the opposite. He knows that by fleeing from fornication, you are causing life to remain in your body. You will have a more abundant life. Death will no longer be your portion.

If you have been sexually immoral and have noticed that some aspects of your life appear to be dead, I want to encourage you that death is not the end for those who believe in Christ. Christians have the free gift of eternal life through Christ.

First Timothy 2:10 says, "... *and which now has been manifested through the appearing of our Savior Christ Jesus, who abolished death and brought life and immortality to light through the gospel.*" Those situations do not have to remain dead in your life anymore.

Christ's death on the cross gifted us with a second chance. Truly repent of your sins and ask God to restore you and bring life to those areas of your life that He intended to flourish. God has many blessings for us, but we must be properly positioned and aligned to receive them.

Many people believe that having sex outside of marriage is a minor sin, so it is no big deal. They clear their conscience by thinking, "At least I'm not committing a big sin like stealing or murdering." This could not be further from the truth. God does not judge sin the same way that most humans do.

First Corinthians 6:9-10 says, "*Or do you not know that the unrighteous will not inherit the kingdom of God? Do not be deceived: neither the sexually immoral, nor idolaters, nor adulterers, nor men who practice homosexuality, nor thieves, nor the greedy, nor drunkards, nor revilers, nor swindlers will inherit the kingdom of God.*"

These verses make no mention of murder. Do you want to gain your inheritance? Why then would you give up your keys to the kingdom for premarital sex? Christ died for your inheritance. A price was paid so you could be set free and inherit the kingdom of God. Do not give it up for a few minutes of pleasure. God desires you to have "*life more abundantly*" (John 10:10).

The Bible reminds us that things that seem small can have a great impact. Song of Solomon 2:15 says, "*Catch all the foxes, those little foxes before they ruin the vineyard of love…*" We should not underestimate the consequences of sexual sin because it seems smaller than other sins. According to this scripture, it is the small things that can ruin a whole big thing. It may be hard to imagine that small foxes can ruin a whole vineyard, but this is true.

Song of Solomon 2:15 creates a great mental image of the impact that small things can make. Pre-marital sex can seem like a menial sin, but it can lead to so much headache, heartbreak, STDs, unplanned pregnancies, guilt, shame, ungodly soul ties, and even death. God wants you to avoid all these things. Therefore, He desires for you to be sexually pure. Beware of those little foxes that can ruin an entire vineyard.

Mastering how to resist sexual temptation while single can prove beneficial even after marriage. Sexual purity is ammunition that you can use in your future marriage. By learning to be disciplined with your sexual desires while you are single, you are planting positive seeds into your future marriage.

If you fell into sexual sin in the past, know that you do not have to live in guilt and shame. Ask God to forgive you of your sins so you can walk in the fullness that He has for you. Ask God to cleanse you from all unrighteousness. Truly repent from your heart and believe you are restored and still valuable. You no longer have to walk in guilt and condemnation for your past sins.

Ephesians 2:4-6 tells us, *"But God, who is rich in mercy, because of His great love with which He loved us, even when we were dead in trespasses, made us alive together with Christ (by grace you have been saved), and raised up together, and made us sit together in the heavenly places in Christ Jesus."* We are indeed restored through Christ!

I pray that you will seriously reflect on the reasons for the importance of sexual purity given in this chapter. I hope they provide a renewed mindset on this topic and allow you to understand sexual purity on a deeper level. God has great desires and plans for your life. I pray that you do not rob yourself of the fullness that God has for you by being sexually impure.

Chapter 11:

God's Intentions for Your Body

I have met many Christians who truly love the Lord but engage in pre-marital sex without guilt or an ounce of conviction. Many Christians believe that the Bible doesn't consider fornication as a sin. However, the Bible speaks against pre-marital sex on different occasions. In this chapter, I will dive a little deeper into what the Bible says about sexual intimacy.

Hebrews 13:4 clearly expresses God's views on sex by saying, *"Honor marriage, and guard the sacredness of sexual intimacy between wife and husband. God draws a firm line against casual and illicit sex."* The Bible is clear. God does not want us to engage in sex that is just casual and illicit.

God views sex between husband and wife as a sacred act. According to the Merriam-Webster dictionary, "sacred" means "dedicated or set apart for the service or worship of a deity." God's desire is for sex to be an act of worship. When two married people engage in sexual intimacy, they are worshipping God.

However, when people who are not married to each other engage in sexual intimacy, they are disobedient to God. This is not worship. It is the opposite of worship. People who engage in sex outside of marriage disregard the sacredness of marriage. It is not an honorable act.

A lot of people make an excuse out of the fact that the desire to engage in sexual intercourse is a natural human desire. They say things like, "God would not give me this desire if He did not want me to act upon it." This mindset can lead people to believe they were created for sex instead of God. We were created to worship God.

Again, the Bible makes God's stance on sexual intimacy clear in First Corinthians 6:13, which says, *"The body is not meant for sexual immorality, but for the Lord, and the Lord for the body."* If you thought that God did not have a problem with you engaging in sex outside of marriage because your body naturally desired it, then I hope this scripture verse dispelled that myth in your life.

I love the example given in the first sentence of First Corinthians 6:13. It is a beautiful simile that says, *"Food is meant for the stomach and the stomach for the food."* God chose to use an example that everyone could relate to. Everyone eats food. It is an integral component of survival.

God is telling us that everything has a specific purpose and a place where it belongs. We shouldn't use things for their intended purpose and in the wrong place. Using things outside of their intended place and purpose could destroy them and make them impossible to use in the future.

Christians are supposed to house the Lord in their bodies. The Lord is supposed to dwell within them. I previously mentioned that this is stated in First Corinthians 6:19, which says, *"Or do you not know that your body is the temple of the Holy Spirit who is in you, whom you have from God, and you are not your own?"*

We should make our bodies a comfortable house for the Lord. Would you want to live in a dirty house? You would feel uncomfortable living in a dirty house, right? So why subject God to that condition while He dwells within you?

Make yourself a comfortable dwelling place for God by keeping your body pure. One aspect of our lives that we can clean out for Christ is our sexual lives. Do a major spring cleaning and get rid of lustful thoughts, ungodly desires, thoughts of homosexuality, movie scenes and lyrics that are displeasing to God, and mental replays of previous sexual encounters.

Deuteronomy 4:24 talks about how God is a jealous God. He wants your WHOLE heart. He wants your life to be pure, holy, and pleasing to Him. He wants to use you. He has BEEN waiting to use you, but you have made no room for Him in your life amongst all of the filth.

When you are expecting guests over to your house, you prepare for them. You do things they would like because you want them to feel comfortable in your home. You want them to enjoy their stay, not leave quickly because they're in a rush to leave the discomfort of your home.

Well, you just learned that your body is a home. Who are you making it comfortable for? God or the devil? Those are the two options. People try to sugarcoat their sins, but it all boils down to whether your actions and the posture of your heart are pleasing to God or the devil.

If your actions are not bringing honor and glory to the kingdom of God, then they are honoring and glorifying the devil. It is that simple. You are either hot, or you're not. In Revelation 3:16, God says, *"But since you are like lukewarm water, neither hot nor cold, I will spit you out of my mouth!"*

I implore you to seriously take the time to consider who you are making your body comfortable for. Is it God or the devil? If it is the devil, repent and ask God to help you clean yourself up while you still have the opportunity. James 4:14 reminds us that tomorrow is not promised.

In First Corinthians 6:19, Paul also mentions, *"Your body is the temple of the Holy Spirit."* For us to fully grasp what Paul means in this statement, we need to understand what a temple is clearly. The Oxford dictionary defines a temple as "a building devoted to the worship of a god or gods."

Who or what is your body devoted to worshipping? As Christians, we should worship the one true living God, the Creator of everything. However, a lot of Christians still haven't devoted their lives and bodies to Him. Being sexually pure is one way that we could devote our bodies to worship God.

When people are not sexually pure, it is obvious that their devotion is elsewhere. If you truly reflect and think deeply about why you do the things you do, you will find where your devotion lies. Some people are devoted to their popularity, favorite celebrity, or significant other.

It is difficult to be entirely devoted to more than one lord. Devotion to God is so much more beneficial than devotion to false gods like people or societal status. Devotion to God prevents us from making mistakes that could lead to extra stress or heartache in our lives.

Truly living for God is such a freeing experience. When you're obedient to God, you can just sit back and watch the positive effects of that obedience manifest. You can be comforted in the fact that if God tells you to do something, then it will be beneficial to you.

There is no need to be anxious about whether the right decision was made. Also, you don't have to wonder whether the consequences of that decision will be favorable. So, what's it going to be? Will you be devoted to the true living God or false gods?

First Corinthians 6:19 also mentions how "you are not your own." The Oxford dictionary defines ownership as "the act, state, or right of possessing something." As a Christian, you don't own your body or life. God has ownership. He paid the price for you.

This may seem scary or oppressive, but God is not that type of owner. He does not beat His children down or treat them like slaves. God loves His children and gives them freedom. God gives us freedom from worry, fear, or any burden. He gives us freedom from sin!

We don't have to pay the price for our sins. He already paid the price for our sins when He died on Calvary. It is an honor and a great privilege not to be your own. The world tries to push the independence agenda, which is ultimately rooted in pride. There are things that every properly functioning human being should be able to do by themselves.

However, the standpoint that you don't need anyone to help you with anything or that you don't want anyone to tell you what to do is deeply rooted in pride. This implies that you think you can do everything and know everything, so you don't need anyone. Where is the humility in that?

Some people struggle to get specific tasks done themselves when they could have asked people for help and accomplished the same tasks more quickly. Some people just want to say they did it all by themselves to impress others. As Christians, our chief objective should not be to glorify ourselves but to glorify God.

God should be getting all of the honor and glory from your life. You can't do anything without Him anyway; your body is not your own. Since our lives belong to God, we should consult Him about what we should be doing with them. Spend time with God to find out His plans for your life.

Find out: Where does He want you to live? Where does He want you to work? Does He even want you to have a traditional job or start your own business? Who does He want you to be in a relationship with (platonic, romantic, business, and spiritual)? Who does He want you to marry?

Does He want you to go to college? Which car does He want you to buy? Which church does He want you to attend? Does He want you to start a church? These questions can continue forever.

I think you get the point. Consult God in EVERY area of your life, with EVERYTHING that you do, and your life will get even better.

"...I ask him to strengthen you through his Spirit - not brute strength, but glorious inner strength - so that Christ can live in you as you open the door and welcome him in. And I ask him that, with both feet planted firmly on love, you'll be able to take in with all followers of Jesus the extravagant dimensions of Christ's love... Live full lives, full in the fullness of God" (Ephesians 3:14-19).

Chapter 12:

Negative Effects of Premarital Sex

Sex is enjoyable and has many benefits, but it also has some unpleasant outcomes. There are many effects of sex in general. However, the consequences of sexual intercourse outside the context of marriage can sometimes be a bit more complex. In this chapter, I will elaborate on some of the general negative effects of fornication.

This chapter is not to condemn anyone who may have encountered any of these examples as a result of premarital sex, but rather to caution people who may not have considered that these things can happen to them. *"There is therefore now no condemnation for those who are in Christ Jesus"* (Romans 8:1).

Unplanned pregnancies

This section does not discourage anyone who may have experienced an unplanned pregnancy. I believe that you can still pursue your dreams and accomplish your goals. Philippians 4:18 says, *"[you] can do everything through Christ, who gives [you] strength."* You can do anything with God's help.

I am just laying out some of the consequences of premarital sex for people who have not seriously considered these consequences. Some people casually have sex as if the consequences are not life-altering, however, they are. It is very important to wait on God's timing to engage in sex. His timing is impeccable, and He explicitly states in His word that His timing for sex is when two people are married to each other.

Unplanned pregnancy is one effect of premarital sex that can completely complicate someone's life. Children are beautiful blessings, but the act of conceiving a child outside of marriage is not something God desires for us. There are indeed several birth control options available. However, it is also true that many people still have unplanned pregnancies. Birth control is not 100% effective. There are numerous circumstances where birth control was used, and pregnancy still ensued.

While babies are a blessing from God, they add responsibility to their parents' lives. They require a lot of finances and time. Women also endure many physical and emotional changes throughout pregnancy and labor. Pregnancy can be a time of joy and excitement, but many people who did not plan to get pregnant can feel sad, anxious, or even ashamed during this time.

Accomplishing lifelong goals can be even harder when you have a child to raise. You have the extra burden of making enough money to provide for yourself and the child, feeding them, disciplining them, taking care of them when they are sick, helping them with homework, etc. Someone with no children does not have all of these things to worry about. They can focus more on God and accomplish their goals.

Proper planning for anything can make that process easier. Raising children is not an exception. If you wait until you have enough money and your life is more stable before you have children, parenting can be much easier. You do not have as much stress and anxiety about providing for them. Also, you can avoid passing this stress on to your children, therefore allowing them to have a less stressful life when you are not always worried about things like finances.

Sometimes single women intentionally become pregnant for various reasons. They may have experienced some failed relationships and feel despondent about getting married. Everyone else in their social circle may have children except them, so they decide that they are tired of waiting until they get married to have children. They want to feel a sense of belonging and accomplishment that comes with having a child.

Some women may even feel that having a child is their opportunity to be completely and purely loved by an individual. They may be longing to feel truly loved, especially if people who they thought truly loved them in the past disappointed or hurt them. However, the baby will be incapable of showing the kind of love that the woman truly desires.

Complete, perfect love can only be found in Christ. The baby will not magically make you feel fulfilled, either. Complete, perfect fulfilment comes from God as well. Children require a lot of work, time, energy, and money. There will be times when they frustrate you far more than they provide you with love, joy, and fulfilment.

Some people also use pregnancy to guilt their partner into remaining in a committed relationship with them. The relationship may be rocky, and they have the view that a child would be able to save the relationship. Often, children make relationships more complicated than they should. Furthermore, children are actual human beings; they should not be pawns.

Your child should not have a job before they are born. Tasking your child with saving your relationship and providing you with fulfilment and love is giving them a job before they can even walk or talk. You don't want to end up miserable and lashing out at your child when they fail to meet your expectations.

Children are a blessing from God, but they require a lot of time, attention, and finances. So many things are easier to do when you don't have to think about caring for a child. For instance, you can travel more often without having to pay for an extra ticket for your child or trying to find someone to babysit your child while you're away.

You can also decide to move to a new country and learn about a new culture without worrying about displacing your child. You have more time to spend on the word of God as well. You could be building yourself up spiritually so that when you have a family to raise, you can do so with a strong spiritual foundation.

Often, people decide to abort the baby or give the baby up for adoption. However, doing these things can have a long-term psychological impact on a person. Birth control may not be 100% effective in protecting against unplanned pregnancies, but abstinence is! The best way to avoid unplanned pregnancies is to not engage in sexual intercourse.

Unhealthy Family Structures

Unplanned pregnancies can lead to unhealthy family structures. One scenario I have witnessed a few times is when a pregnancy happens due to an extramarital affair. If the parent decides to remain in the marriage, the child can feel like they do not belong or even feel rejected. They may compare their lives to the lives of their siblings that were conceived during the marriage.

The child could grow up with resentment in their hearts towards the parent or their siblings. Even in instances where this type of situation is handled with maturity, there can still be complications that arise. The child who was born outside of the marriage may still have a feeling of abandonment or experience low self-esteem.

There are also instances where one parent abandons the child because they cannot handle the responsibility of raising a child. When this happens, the child may feel rejected and unwanted. They may feel like their parents abandoned them because there is something wrong with them that makes them too difficult to love.

Soul Ties

A soul tie is a strong emotional connection between individuals. It is mentioned in the Bible in First Samuel 18:1. This verse states, "*... the soul of Jonathan was knit to the soul of David, and Jonathan loved him as his own soul.*" Soul ties can be formed between people who are very emotionally or physically intimate with each other. David and Jonathan were good friends, so they had an emotional soul tie with each other.

Soul ties can be healthy or unhealthy. If the relationship is stable and God-ordained, then the soul tie is healthy. If the relationship is unstable and dysfunctional and God did not ordain it, then the soul tie may be unhealthy.

One of the quickest and easiest ways for a soul tie to form between two people is when they engage in sexual intercourse. When a husband and wife form a soul tie in this way, it is seen as a healthy soul tie. However, sexual soul ties formed outside of marriage can be quite unhealthy. Marriage is a lifetime commitment; therefore, it is beneficial for husbands and wives to be soul tied to each other.

When two unmarried people form sexual soul ties to each other, it may cause them to be spiritually connected to someone they are not best suited for. It is hard for them to leave the relationship, even if it is toxic.

The couple may try to part ways but end up reconnecting because they did not break the soul tie. The soul tie makes it difficult for them to end the relationship. This can leave a lot of people feeling stuck, stupid, or confused. This can also cause people to waste time in relationships unnecessarily.

Soul ties can also cause people to take on the problems of the people to whom they are soul tied. For instance, someone may not have a history of depression. However, after being sexually intimate with someone who has that struggle, they may begin to struggle with depression. Spiritual transfers are not uncommon with soul ties. This is why it is important to only be sexually intimate with someone who God ordains for your life and at the right time after you are married.

God knows what you are graced to handle. He knows the struggles that your husband or wife may be enduring, and He knows that you will have the grace to help them through those struggles. This is why it is so important to earnestly seek God about who to marry. Somebody may look like the perfect package from your point of view, but God can see everything about that person. God can see things that you cannot. He has the perfect, full view. He also knows the battles that He equipped you to overcome.

Many people are having a hard time in life because they are fighting battles that are not theirs. They are dealing with predicaments that God never meant for them because they are soul tied to the wrong people. They struggle with things like depression, anxiety, or low self-esteem, which their sexual partners pick up. They must be free of those soul ties and everything that goes with them. Life can present its challenges. Therefore, you do not need to pick up the challenges of others along the way.

When two people engage in sexual intercourse, hug, kiss, or bond socially, a hormone called oxytocin is released. This hormone encourages pair bonding and causes people to have an overly optimistic view of the other person they have had intimate contact with. They see these people in a better light than they actually are. You cannot effectively discern a person's character if you only have an overly optimistic view of them.

If you have formed any unhealthy soul ties in the past or are currently in one now, you could break them by asking God for forgiveness and asking Him to break the soul tie. Truly be sincere and repent. Sometimes, people want a soul tie broken solely because they want their feelings for another person to stop. The type of repentance is not genuine because they are not convicted about engaging in premarital sex; they just want their broken heart to recover.

It is also wise to get rid of anything the person gave you. Those things will only remind you of the person and rekindle feelings towards them that you are trying to let go of. Simply looking at these items can bring up old memories that you should not dwell on.

I implore you to be careful with your soul and your emotional well-being. While contraceptives can protect your physical body, they cannot protect you emotionally and spiritually. The best way to fully protect your body is to refrain from sexual intercourse until you are married to the person whom God ordained for you to marry.

Hurt/Pain

Another negative effect of premarital sex can be the hurt or pain that results from giving your body to someone who does not truly value it. Sometimes, people give someone extra attention and say nice things to them just to lure them into having sex. However, once the sexual experience is over, all of the good treatment ends.

Most of the time, once the person has gotten what he wants, he breaks up with them or stops pursuing them. In many cases, there was no real relationship to start with. One person was holding onto the dream that constant communication could lead to a relationship, while the other person just wanted constant communication to lead to sex.

This can leave the person who wanted the relationship feeling rejected, used, and hurt. Their self-esteem may even suffer, and they may lose hope of ever being in a serious romantic relationship. There have been instances where people in this situation decide to project that pain on others by using other people for sex so they can feel empowered.

Guess what? All of this unnecessary pain can be avoided by choosing to be abstinent until marriage. When you decide not to engage in pre-marital sex, you naturally get rid of all of the people who solely want to have a sexual relationship. You can also get to know someone better because your judgment is not clouded by the oxytocin released during sex. You can make a better-informed decision about whether you should continue dating someone because you can discern their character more effectively.

STDs

Sexually Transmitted Diseases are another unpleasant result of pre-marital sex. For some reason, many people believe they will not contract an STD from the person they are engaging in sexual intercourse with. I don't know how they came to that conclusion especially as STDs are not written on people's faces. You might want to use their appearances as a judge, but I kid you not, you never can tell. Many attractive, intelligent, and successful people have STDs.

You cannot determine whether a person has an STD by simply looking at them, no matter how your hormones are making you feel about them. While different types of contraceptives are available that decrease the risk of spreading STDs, they cannot fully prevent transmission. Even when using contraceptives, you are still at risk of contracting an STD, and people have contracted STDs while using contraceptives.

Some STDs are incurable; therefore, people must deal with them for the rest of their lives. A few minutes of pleasure gave them a lifelong disease. STDs can lead to infertility, cancers, sores, rashes, painful urination, and painful sexual encounters. Also, people with STDs have the additional expense of purchasing medication to treat the symptoms.

Suppose you engaged in pre-marital sex in the past, and the result was an unplanned pregnancy, soul ties, a broken heart, contracting a sexually transmitted disease, or any other unpleasant result. In that case, you are still valuable in God's sight. You don't have to give up on your walk with God or even give up on living a sexually pure life.

Lamentations 3:23 talks about how God's "*mercies begin afresh each morning*." This means God has more compassion and forgiveness to extend to you every morning. His mercy does not run out, no matter how many mistakes you make. Don't allow the enemy to lie to you and convince you that you have sinned too much to have a relationship with God or attain purity.

As long as you breathe, you are qualified to receive God's grace and mercy. I watched a sermon by Michael Todd the other day where he mentioned that God's grace is sufficient, but you may end up with scars that you wouldn't have otherwise. It is important to remember that our actions have consequences. Although God's grace is sufficient and His mercy is abounding, we should still act in wisdom.

Chapter 13:

So, you want to get married just to have sex?

The story I'm about to share with you is relevant to anyone considering marriage for the sake of sex or fleeting feelings. I do not want you to be in the same predicament as the story's main characters, Julia and Cameron. You may be someone who has not had sex for a while or never had sex at all because you are practicing abstinence.

You meet someone to whom you are physically attracted, and you're so overcome by hormones and the fact that you have been without sex for a long time that you decide to skip the normal dating process to avoid having sex outside of marriage.

Julia and Cameron met at a church picnic. Cameron asked Julia on a date the following week, and they felt like they had hit it off. The conversation was incredible, and they had a lot of surface-level things in common, like their spiritual beliefs, work ethic, music, and food. They both felt like they had met their lifelong partner.

Julia and Cameron were physically attracted to each other. Most of their conversations and interactions were dominated by this physical attraction and even became lustful. Although they both decided that they wanted to wait until marriage to have sex, they did other things to act on their physical attraction.

A lot of their conversations were impure. During some late-night phone calls, Cameron played romantic music in the background and spoke in a sultry voice. Also, there were conversations where Julia made it clear that she was not a virgin and always knew how to please her man in the bedroom before becoming a Christian. There were instances where she elaborated on the details.

Julia and Cameron had fit, attractive bodies and dressed provocatively to show off their physiques. This heightened the feelings of lust they had toward each other. There would be instances when she and Cameron were hanging out alone together, and things got very heated. They pretty much did everything except have sex. There were no physical boundaries in their relationship except for sex.

One day, after dating for two months, Cameron decides to propose to Julia. He felt like he had found the one whom he should spend the rest of his life with. Elated, Julia accepts the proposal, and they begin planning their wedding. They decide to have a short engagement because they are so sure that they are supposed to spend the rest of their lives together.

After meeting with their pastor, he advises them to get to know each other a little more before deciding to marry. They found it difficult to answer questions about whether they wanted children, their parenting styles, and their finances. This is because they have never really talked about these things before. During the two months they had been dating, they mainly talked about highlights of their day, movies and television shows, stories about their past, and things they wished they could do to each other sexually.

Their friends and family shared the same sentiments as their pastor. They thought that Cameron and Julia should take more time to get to know each other. Julia's family was especially upset that they never got to meet Cameron until after they were already engaged. Since they did not have much support from their family and friends, they decided to go to the park, where they met and had a small private wedding.

So, you want to get married just to have sex?

The first few months of their marriage were pure bliss. They had sex constantly, they spent a lot of time with each other, and their disagreements did not last longer than a day. However, after six months of marriage, things changed. The honeymoon phase was over, and the spark was not there anymore.

They started to get annoyed with each other and had more frequent disagreements that lasted much longer than before. They began to learn things about each other that they did not know before. For instance, Julia had a serious spending problem.

Julia's spending did not seem like a big deal to Cameron initially, but he did not realize how much of a problem it was until he bought a new car. His car was experiencing mechanical issues that were quite costly to fix. When he checked their account, he found out that a lot of money was missing.

He knew Julia shopped frequently, but he did not realize how much she was spending on these shopping trips. Julia was annoyed with Cameron because she thought he was a slob who did not know how to clean up after himself. She felt like she was becoming a maid. Going to work all day and then returning home to cook and clean after a grown man was becoming draining and annoying.

Julia became a nag for Cameron. She constantly complained about what he left on the floor or forgot to clean. She thought that if she constantly reminded him to do things, he would eventually do them. However, this method was not very effective. Cameron did not do the things she kept pestering him about, and her nagging pushed him away.

Cameron started coming home from work later and spent a lot more time out with his friends than with Julia. When he was home, he seemed distant. He was not enthusiastic about spending time with his wife. One day, he told Julia that he didn't think he was in love with her anymore. He told her that their pastors, friends, and family were right. They should not have gotten married so soon.

Julia was crushed and asked him to consider marriage counseling before going their separate ways. Cameron agreed. Unfortunately, counseling made things worse. After a few months of trying, they decided to end the marriage. Their chemistry and physical attraction were not enough to make their marriage last. They were too different. Their lives were fundamentally going in different directions.

I hope Julia and Cameron's story made you aware of some of the dangers of getting married to have sex and how you end up in that sort of marriage. Cameron and Julia did not think that they were getting married for sex; they believed they were in love. A lot of signs indicated that they were in lust, not love; however, they could not see it.

While it is honorable to be desirous of waiting until marriage to have sex, rushing the wait can have unfavorable repercussions. I know that waiting patiently when you have sexual urges can be hard. That is why the next few chapters are dedicated to sharing sexual purity tips. However, in this chapter, I want to share how you could avoid ending up in a situation like Cameron and Julia, who got married just to have sex.

One of the reasons why I pointed out the difference between sexual purity and sexual abstinence earlier in this book is that it is helpful when dating. When you are only trying to be sexually abstinent until marriage, you and your partner can end up doing other sexually impure things other than sex. When your goal is to be sexually pure, you're not just abstaining from sex but also other sexually impure behaviors.

For instance, someone who is sexually pure would not sext (send sexually explicit messages via cellphone), fondle, have lustful or enticing conversations about sex, or have long passionate kissing sessions. Pursuing sexual purity instead of just abstinence is one thing that will help you avoid getting married just to have sex.

Serious praying and fasting about whether you should marry someone and seeking wise counsel from spiritual leaders, family, and friends who love and care about you are also vital to avoid the heartache of marrying the wrong person. I do not necessarily believe that the length of time in which Julia and Cameron dated was the main error, but the oversight can be found in what they were doing in the two months that they were dating.

Some people who date for a short period have strong, long marriages. However, during the brief time they dated, they were intentional, focused, and desired to honor God and one another.

They got to know each other. They spent time with each other's family and friends and talked about their strong beliefs and life plans. Sometimes, two friends who have known each other for years decide to date for a short period before getting married because they already know so much about each other.

On the other hand, there could be people who date for years but are unsuitable for marriage. Their long-dating relationship works because they haven't made any big decisions together and still have individual lives. However, if the two lives had to merge, it would be a disaster. In this situation, serious prayer and wise counsel would help the couple make the best marriage decision.

Determining whether love exists in the relationship can also help you evaluate whether you should marry someone or the right time to marry them. My favorite definition of love can be found in the Bible in First Corinthians 13.

The New King James Version of First Corinthians 13 says:

"Though I speak with the tongues of men and of angels, but have not love, I have become sounding brass or a clanging cymbal. [2] *And though I have the gift of prophecy, and understand all mysteries and all*

knowledge, and though I have all faith, so that I could remove mountains, but have not love, I am nothing. [3] *And though I bestow all my goods to feed the poor, and though I give my body to be burned, but have not love, it profits me nothing.*

[4] *Love suffers long and is kind; love does not envy; love does not parade itself, is not puffed up;* [5] *does not behave rudely, does not seek its own, is not provoked, thinks no evil;* [6] *does not rejoice in iniquity, but rejoices in the truth;* [7] *bears all things, believes all things, hopes all things, endures all things.*

[8] *Love never fails. But whether there are prophecies, they will fail; whether there are tongues, they will cease; whether there is knowledge, it will vanish away.* [9] *For we know in part and we prophesy in part.* [10] *But when that which is perfect has come, then that which is in part will be done away.*

[11] *When I was a child, I spoke as a child, I understood as a child, I thought as a child; but when I became a man, I put away childish things.* [12] *For now we see in a mirror, dimly, but then face to face. Now I know in part, but then I shall know just as I also am known.*

[13] *And now abide faith, hope, love, these three; but the greatest of these is love."*

This chapter can help you formulate questions to ask yourself to determine whether you truly love someone or if they truly love you.

You can ask:

Is the person patient?

Is the person kind?

Is this person envious or boastful?

Are they arrogant or rude?

Does this person always insist on having their way?

Is this person irritable or resentful?

So, you want to get married just to have sex?

Does this person celebrate wrongdoing?
Does this person celebrate the truth?
Can this person hope for all things?
Can this person endure all things?

Ask these questions of yourself and your love interest. Take responsibility for yourself before attempting to pass it on to someone else.

I am not saying that if the answer is not favorable to all these questions, it means the person does not genuinely love you, or you don't truly love them. Nobody is perfect, and if we are honest with ourselves, we all have room for growth when it comes to love. However, have these things even been considered? Is there a willingness to grow in deficient areas?

Understanding the sacredness and importance of marriage can also help to prevent you from getting married for the wrong reasons. The Bible has several scriptures that reveal the gravity of marriage. There is a lot of power that husbands and wives have in their spouses' lives that people do not realize.

Ephesians 5 provides some examples of the severity of marriage. Verse 22 says, "*Wives, submit to your own husbands, as to the Lord.*" This is a serious instruction for wives. It causes women to realize they should marry someone they want to submit to.

This statement alone will cause women to truly get to know a man's character before deciding to marry him. Ladies, is this man someone who you can trust and truly see yourself submitting to for the rest of your life? Don't marry a jerk, then get mad because you don't want to submit to his jerk ways.

Another verse that alerts us of the severity of marriage is Ephesians 5:25. This verse instructs men. It says, "*Husbands, love your wives just as Christ also loved the church and gave Himself for her.*" This is no easy, flaky, emotional kind of love. Christ truly and authentically loved the church because He died for the church.

In marriage, you may not have to die physically, but there will be moments when you have to die to your flesh for your wife's sake. This will not be comfortable because you would be giving up your wants and desires for the sake of another human being. I could imagine that practicing this level of selflessness can be extremely difficult.

These selfless acts lead to the husband's ability to *"sanctify and cleanse [his wife] with the washing of water by the word"* (Ephesians 5:26). This is an important scripture for both men and women to know. Men should be well versed in scripture since they are required to cleanse their wives with it.

Also, women should choose to marry a man who is well versed in scripture so he can cleanse her with it. If a husband is not cleansing his wife with the Word of God, he may be making her filthy with whatever else is in him.

Some men only know a few verses but obey them and live according to them. They are also capable of sanctifying and cleansing their wives with the Word in a kind, gentle, and effective way.

On the other hand, some men know a lot of scripture, but their lives don't reflect their biblical knowledge, and they are not gentle with their sanctification and cleansing methods. They use the sword to pierce into the soul and spirits of their wives violently. They feel justified in this because they think it is their husbandly duty. Abrasive cleaning can lead to long-term damage.

Firefighters are trained to use high-pressure hoses because they know the damage that even water can do when not used properly. Although water is a cleanser, it can do more harm than good if not used with wisdom. Men, I implore you to be gracious with your wives as you wash them with the Word of God.

Ask God to grant you wisdom and discernment to execute this cleansing process effectively. Wash your wife with the Word, not drown her. This would create serious problems in your marriage if not done the right way. However, if executed with grace, wisdom, and love, it can cause your marriage to flourish.

Another verse that reveals the gravity of marriage is Ephesians 5:31. It says, "*A man shall leave his father and mother and be joined to his wife, and the two shall become one flesh.*" You are becoming one with the person you choose to marry. Your body, thoughts, emotions, goals, dreams, and plans are intertwined. You cannot make major decisions without taking your partner into account. The things you do seriously affect your partner as well.

Just think about it for a minute. Your finances, health, and where you live, work, and eat all affect your partner. There are so many other things that I could add to this list. Marriage truly forces you to be more considerate and accommodating. You do not want to be one flesh with the wrong person as that will make life so much more difficult, and your marriage will feel like a miserable trap.

Sometimes, people remain in relationships with or even marry the wrong person because they look great on paper. Technically, there is nothing wrong with them, but it seems like something is missing. This person may be great and a blessing to anyone who is in a relationship with them, but they are just not the right person for you.

It is important to pray if you're in a situation like this, and if God is leading you to end the relationship, then you should end it. You may crush that person's feelings, but they will get over it and hopefully meet the person who is better suited for them. As you can see from the scriptural examples that I pointed out, marriage is a serious deal, and you should not marry anyone just because they look good on paper or you enjoy being in each other's company.

Some people are better suited for helping you fulfill your purpose on this earth than others. Therefore, it would be easier to become one flesh with them. God would have already equipped them with the skills and even the personality to walk through life with you. Patience is key. Patience will prevent you from making the mistakes that come with rushing the process. Marriage is a lifetime commitment, so take your time and choose wisely.

After you say, "I do," you don't instantly become blind and stop noticing attractive people. You will continue to meet physically appealing people who may even be attracted to you. Temptation can arise to act upon your mutual physical attraction. However, people who were sexually pure during their season of singleness have extra ammunition to help them resist temptation.

Just as a gun needs ammunition to be successful at hitting a target, your spiritual being needs ammunition to help you succeed at anything in life, including marriage. You can use the discipline learned during a season of abstinence as ammunition to fire whenever you are in a tempting situation.

People who practiced abstinence before are knowledgeable on how to deny themselves and starve their sexual appetite successfully, and there was a period when they practiced this continuously. Marriage can have its fair share of challenges and hurdles. It would be wise to go into it with extra ammunition. Sexual purity is helpful for singles and married couples alike.

There are so many verses in the Bible that talk about marriage, and I encourage you to study them. Some scriptures are Genesis 2:23-24, Matthew 19:4-6, Colossians 3:18, and Hebrews 13:4.

I truly believe that I make wiser choices when it comes to dating because I took the time to study what the Bible says about marriage. It took me a few months to study this topic because I was really taking my time and digesting what the Bible has to say in small portions.

This is not a Bible study you can thoroughly complete in a day, but it is worth every moment. Knowing what the Bible says about marriage can help you quickly identify red flags in a dating relationship. Especially if your long-term goal for dating or courting is a God-centered marriage.

I pray that you seriously consider what God's Word says about marriage before going into a marriage for the wrong reasons. I pray that God gives you the patience and wisdom to wait purely. May you enjoy your single season and take advantage of everything it has to offer. I pray that your ultimate life satisfaction is pleasing God and not marriage.

May the Lord grant you the wisdom and discernment to marry the right person when the time is right. If you have been married before or suffered from a difficult breakup, I pray that God completely heals all your wounds and restores you. I pray that you receive God's peace, love, and rejuvenation.

Chapter 14:

Prayer & Fasting

One quote that I love by Joyce Meyer is, "Patience is not the ability to wait, but how you act while you're waiting." I struggled with patience for a long time. To be honest, I still have moments of weakness when it comes to patience. This quote helped me to analyze my actions and thoughts when I am put in situations where I am required to wait.

There were instances where I was trying to be patient, but I was annoyed and complained while I waited. This quote helped me to realize the magnitude of what patience consists of. It's not simply waiting for something or someone, but having a positive attitude while waiting.

We shouldn't be bitter, worried, upset, and ungrateful while we are waiting. It is so important to be self-aware and to notice when you don't have the right attitude when it comes to waiting and adjust your actions accordingly.

Many people will not be single for their entire lives. Their single season can be viewed as a waiting season for marriage. Some people wait impurely during their single season. However, this does not have to be the case. In this chapter and the following chapters, I will be unpacking some tools from my sexual purity toolbox that have tips for remaining sexually pure during the season of singleness.

I need to note that none of these tips could be accomplished without the power of the Holy Spirit. Firstly, I would not have had the wisdom to use any of these tips if the Holy Spirit had not revealed them to me. Secondly, I would not be able to successfully practice these tips if the Holy Spirit did not grant me the discipline to do so. By God's power and strength, I am sexually pure and will remain a virgin until I am married.

My biggest tip for remaining pure is PRAYER. Prayer produces purity. When I decided that I wanted to remain a virgin until marriage, I prayed for God to help me to accomplish this goal. I knew that I could not do it on my own. This should be a constant prayer in the lives of single Christians, especially if you foresee yourself being in a predicament where you are tempted more than usual.

Your sexual purity prayer doesn't have to be elaborate when you are starting. Your prayer can be as simple as this, "Dear Heavenly Father, please help me to be sexually pure. In Jesus Christ's name, I pray. Amen." Easy enough, right? You can add to this prayer by asking God to remove any impure thoughts from your mind and replace them with pure thoughts.

You can also ask God to remove your desire to engage in sex until you are married. You can ask Him to replace those desires with His pure desires for your life at this time. Another request you can make is for the Lord to cover your mind and your heart so no impure thoughts infiltrate them throughout the day.

You can ask God to provide you with strategies to remain sexually pure. After praying this prayer, wait for God to respond with strategies. He may tell you the strategies plainly right away, or He may lead you to resources that contain tips for sexual purity. You may also feel a check in your spirit to stop doing something or find that you don't fully enjoy doing it anymore. This can be God answering your prayer by convicting you about doing things that can lead to a sexually impure lifestyle.

After praying, remember to be patient with yourself. You may still have slip-up instances, especially if your body is already acclimated to having sex often. Do not give up if you do have slip-ups. Continue to pray about it and ask God to help you to get back on the right track.

After a while, you will find that you are improving at resisting temptation. God sees that you are trying and will honor you for your efforts to remain pure. Eventually, you will have a beautiful testimony of being delivered from fornication, and you will be able to help others in their purity journey.

There are some seasons where sexual temptation is stronger than in other seasons. I increased my sexual purity prayers before going to college. I could foresee myself being tempted on a college campus by smart, attractive men.

I would not have accountability from my parents, as I would no longer be living with them. Also, many college campuses are filled with the spirit of lust. Many young people living on college campuses are attracted to each other, and they tend to act on that attraction by having sex with each other.

I am grateful that God answered my prayers during that season. Although there were temptations and opportunities to fornicate, I remained a virgin. I could not have accomplished this without the help of the Holy Spirit guiding me and providing me with wisdom. I am a testimony that sexual purity prayers work, and it is possible to refrain from fornication.

Prayer and fasting are a beautiful combination. The battle to be sexually pure attacks the flesh. As Christians, we need to learn to die to our flesh. We have become so accustomed to living according to our feelings that we do the same thing with our sex lives. If you struggle with self-discipline or dying to your flesh, I implore you to go on a fast.

Fasting causes you to be more self-disciplined because you refuse to give the body what it wants. A lot of people are not self-disciplined because it does not feel good to discipline their flesh. When you are fasting from food, it does not feel good to deny your body food and be hungry. However, if you often fast, your body adjusts to being without food, and hunger will not feel so dreadful.

Different fasts last for different lengths of time. You can go on a total fast where you do not consume any food or liquids. You can also partake in fasts where you do not eat food but drink only liquids. There are also fasts where you do not eat any meat.

Furthermore, you can fast by skipping a certain meal or meals throughout the day and using the time you would usually eat to spend with God. I suggest you search for fasting resources to help you choose the best fast for your lifestyle. There are additional resources that will expound on how to start and break a fast properly so you do not harm your body. It is also wise to consult your medical doctor before partaking in a fast.

The Bible mentions some important information about fasting. Matthew 6:16-18 talks about how we should not let everyone know when we are fasting. Fasting should be kept private between God and us. If we were to let everyone know, then our reward would be the fact that everyone knows we are fasting. If we keep our fasting a secret, then God will reward us openly.

Matthew 6:17-18 says, *"But you, when you fast, anoint your head and wash your face, so that you do not appear to men to be fasting, but to your Father who is in the secret place; and your Father who sees in secret will reward you openly."*

God gives us these instructions for fasting because He wants to ensure we are fasting from a pure heart. If you are fasting to be seen and think you are doing a good deed, then you have missed the point of fasting. You should be fasting so you can grow in your relationship with God, not so you can grow in your popularity with humans.

It makes perfect sense that if you were fasting to please men, then you would receive your end goal, the admiration of men.

However, if you are fasting for God, then your end goal would be to please God, and God will reward you. Always make sure you are fasting with pure motives.

You may notice your flesh begins to rise during the fast. You may feel a heightening of sexual urges or other sinful habits during your fast. That is normal. Fasting usually brings our sins to the forefront so we can deal with them. If you notice this happening to you, pray about it and know that it means you are closer to your breakthrough.

A major aspect of fasting is spending more time with God, so you are filling yourself up spiritually. Although your physical body is suffering, you are growing spiritually and more prepared for life's battles. After I began to fast more often, I noticed that it was easier to die to my flesh.

I also found it easier to be disciplined in other areas of my life while fasting. Dying to my flesh has become more normal and less unbearable. Going without something your body needs, like food, will teach your body discipline to go without other things your body tells you to need, like sex.

I implore you to take advantage of prayer and fasting. These are life-changing tools, not only for sexual purity but in other areas of your spiritual life as well. Fasting may not be easy, but you will notice that it helps you to be a more disciplined believer. It will also improve your intimacy with God.

Fasting is a useful tool that can be used to remain sexually pure, however, there is more that can be done to maintain a sexually pure lifestyle. Ephesians 6:11 (ESV) is an encouragement to *"Put on the whole armor of God, that you may be able to stand against the schemes of the devil."* A lot of people do not view sexual urges as attacks of the devil because they are natural. However, they are attacks from the devil when that sexual desire is not for your husband or wife. It is an attack on your spiritual life because God calls us to be sexually pure.

On the surface, the person you are attracted to can be the primary source of your sexual difficulties; however, it is much deeper than that. Ephesians 6:12 (NKJV) says, *"For we do not wrestle against flesh and blood, but against principalities, against powers, against the rulers of the darkness of this age, against spiritual hosts of wickedness in heavenly places."*

I know this verse can seem scary and confusing. However, it is saying that humans are not the ones we should be trying to overcome or defeat. Flesh and blood in this verse represent human beings. Humans may physically represent that temptation; however, a spiritual battle occurs.

There is an order to the spiritual world. Although demons orchestrate a lot of chaos in the world, they have a certain order amongst themselves. They have rankings in the spiritual realm. Similar to how governments have a ranking order, demons also have a ranking order, and their rank dictates how much power they have.

Ephesians 6:12 mentions three different levels within the demonic spiritual leadership; principalities, powers, and rulers of the darkness. Principalities are high-ranking spiritual beings who direct demons on which tasks to complete. Powers are demonic officials that rank below principalities. Rulers of the darkness are demonic leaders who are less powerful than powers.

Often, people lose the battle against the enemy because their strategy is flawed. They decide to cut off the person who is causing them to lust. They can also stop looking at lustful images, or even stop watching pornography. These are great things to do. I encourage doing these things in this book. However, doing these things does not mean that you have won the battle.

These things can be considered an aspect of the battle, but the battle itself is spiritual. Instead of just praying to stop looking at people lustfully, you can go a step deeper and pray against the spirits that are causing you to lust. You can ask God to command heavenly angels to wage war against the demonic powers that are trying to cause you to fall into temptation.

Second Corinthians 10:3-4 (NKJV) states, *"For though we walk in the flesh, we do not war according to the flesh. For the weapons of our warfare are not carnal but mighty in God for pulling down strongholds."* This scripture is encouraging us to fight the battle against the enemy spiritually. Although we are humans, the battle that we are in is not in the human form.

This is why prayer and fasting are so essential. When we truly start praying against the spiritual forces that are coming up against us, we can overcome them. We can also pray for divine help, and God can send His angels to fight on our behalf. An example of this is seen in Daniel 10:13 (AMP), which says, *"But the prince of the kingdom of Persia was standing in opposition to me for twenty-one days. Then, behold, Michael, one of the chiefs [of the celestial] princes, came to help me, for I had been left there with the kings of Persia."*

An angel came to assist Daniel during his time of great need. For twenty-one days, a demonic force opposed him. Once the angel of the Lord came, Daniel was able to move. Angels are powerful heavenly beings that can fight on our behalf. While it is important not to worship angels because God is the ultimate power and King, we can use their assistance when we are in need.

I guarantee you that once you start seeing this battle for what it is, a spiritual battle, and use the correct strategies to defeat the enemy, then you will be victorious against the schemes of the devil. Thinking about the demonic spiritual activity may seem scary. However, you have no reason to fear. If you are a Christian, you are already on the winning side. There is no being that is more powerful than God. All you have to do is call upon God for assistance in your time of trouble.

Chapter 15:
Relationships Matter

A good sexual purity tool is understanding your self-worth. I talked about this earlier in this book, but I would like to briefly remind you. Many people give up on their purity commitment to God to please someone that they are interested in. You are far more valuable than that. If someone requires sex to be in a relationship with you, then they are not the right fit for you. Your hope and identity should be in Christ, not in whether you can get or keep a man or woman.

Also, someone does not fully respect your body if they want to have sex with you outside of marriage. Your partner should treat you as someone precious. They should know that your body belongs to God, and engaging in premarital sex is not only disrespectful to you but disrespectful to God. God clearly instructs us not to have sex until marriage in His word through scriptures like First Thessalonians 4:3. This scripture says, *"For this is the will of God, even your sanctification, that ye should abstain from fornication."*

You should also be in a romantic relationship with someone who realizes that you have so much more to offer than sex. Your partner should understand that it is a great privilege to be with you because of your mind, personality, passions in life, drive, character, etc.

Instead of thinking less of you because you are not willing to have sex outside of marriage, they should think more highly of you because you want to wait. They should see sexual abstinence as something to be valued. Someone who God has not convicted about sex outside of marriage does not fully understand why it is important. They may be offended by your refusal to have sex with them.

They may consider that a form of rejection and use that to manipulate you and make you feel guilty for not indulging in sex. This can add a lot of unnecessary stress and strain to the relationship. It is much easier to be involved with someone who has the same convictions and spiritual beliefs as you.

Also, it is much more difficult to remain sexually pure if you are in a relationship with someone who does not have that same goal. All the pressure would lie on you to uphold your purity standards. This is why it is important to talk about sexual purity early in a romantic relationship.

If you have the same sexual purity goals, you could be comforted that you are on the same page in that area of your life. If that person does not have the same purity goals as you, then you are aware early on in the relationship. Both of you can decide whether or not you want to continue the relationship before you become too attached.

If your significant other has the same spiritual beliefs as you regarding sex, it will be easier for both of you to be sexually abstinent before marriage. You would be able to pray about the boundaries God wants you to set in your relationship so you can remain sexually pure. You can also hold each other accountable, so the pressure would not always be on one person to ensure that the two of you are not giving in to temptation.

You may think that it is not a big deal if your partner is not pursuing sexual purity, but it is. Even if they say they will honor your decision to abstain from sex, complications may still arise in the relationship. They may grow tired of waiting and try to convince you to have sex with them. This can make you feel guilty or less valuable because you will not fulfill your partner's desire.

Or your partner may slip up and have sex with someone else. Even if they are faithful to you, you may think in the back of your head that they will be unfaithful because you know they desire to have sex. You may think they are getting their sexual needs met by someone else, which can create unnecessary distrust in the relationship.

Your significant other may try to manipulate you or convince you to change your mind about having sex. They may even make you feel guilty about not having sex with them. Not only are these signs of an unhealthy relationship, but they are also signs that you are not compatible spiritually.

What would happen if you two were to get married and have children? Is this person capable of instilling good Christian values into your children, or will they be an example of someone who believes in God but is lukewarm in their relationship with God? There are enough examples of people like that in society. Your children do not need to see that in their parents as well.

It is very special and profound when someone is so serious about their devotion to God that they want to abstain from sex until marriage. It shows a certain level of spiritual maturity that is admirable. This level of devotion and discipline can prove to be beneficial in other areas of life. If someone is not devoted enough to God, whom they claim to love more than anything else, what level of devotion do you expect them to give you?

If they end up being more devoted to you than they are to God, this can be very dangerous because it means you have become their idol. Human beings make terrible idols. You cannot fully satisfy their every need as only God can. They can never find wholeness in you. They would expect things from you that you cannot give, and the relationship would be toxic.

It is important to have like-minded friends in general. Do not worry about the people who are telling you that you are "being extra," or "doing too much," or "it doesn't take all of that." If God has instructed you to do something or convicted you about something that you have been doing, then be obedient. Everyone is different, so they have different boundaries.

Your relationship with God should be just that—a relationship between you and God. It is great to receive good Godly counsel to help you grow closer to Him. However, many people allow the opinions of others to create distance between them and God. God told them to do something, but because popular opinion disagrees, they decide not to do it. Or God tells them not to do something, but other people disagree, so they decide to do it anyway.

Romans 8:38 says, "*Nothing can ever separate us from God's love,*" and this is very true. Nothing that we do can stop God from loving us. However, our actions can determine how deep our relationship with God can be. Disobedience destroys depth. Disobedience is one action that can kill depth in our relationship with God.

Isaiah 59:2 says, "*But your iniquities have separated you from your God; And your sins have hidden His face from you, So that He will not hear.*" This verse proves that our actions can create distance in our relationship with God.

When a young adult decides to move out of the house, they create distance between themselves and their parents. The parents still love their child, who has decided to move out of the house. However, their relationship would not be as strong as it was when they lived at home. There is a strain in the relationship because there is less interaction among them.

The child who moved out also does not have the same benefits they had when living with their parents. They may have more freedom to do whatever they choose. However, freedom has a cost. The child now has to pay all of their bills. This child may have also benefited from the groceries their parents bought and the meals their parents prepared, but now they have to purchase groceries and cook all of their meals.

The same thing happens when we sin against God. We move out of the intimate place that we have with Him. He still loves us, but we are too far away from Him to reap the full benefits of intimacy with the Father. It may seem like we have more freedom, but this supposed freedom has costs. It can cost us not to experience the fullness of what God has for us.

Any relationship requires sacrifices. You cannot always expect to do things your way. God made the first and ultimate sacrifice in your relationship with Him by sending His only son to die on the cross for your sins. He started your relationship with a very dynamic and unconventional sacrifice. So why not sacrifice some things for Him?

Your friends may not understand, but God is worth it. People may make fun of you and call you extra, but a relationship with God is so worth it. You may lose friends, boyfriends, or girlfriends because of your obedience to God, but trust me when I say your relationship with God is more than worth it. God is the best life partner that you could ever have. Your relationship with God is the greatest and most beneficial relationship that you could ever be in.

The type of friends you associate with plays a key role in your sexually pure lifestyle. Your friends have the power to influence you toward purity or away from it. First Corinthians 5:9 says, "*... you shouldn't make yourselves at home among the sexually promiscuous.*" If your friends do not see a problem with engaging in pre-marital sex, you can begin to develop some internal struggles with it and over time, fall into a temptation that you wouldn't have fallen into if you cut those ties off.

You should have friends who can help hold you accountable to your commitments to God. Your friends should encourage you to pursue purity, not treat you like something is wrong with you because you are abstinent. There is already enough opposition and misunderstanding from around the world. Your friendships should be your safe space and encourage you to mature in the things of God.

I did not graduate from a Christian high school, so my classmates thought I was a super Christian. Honestly, when I look back on my walk with God now, I can say that it was not very great. I had a fragile relationship with God. I loved Him and knew that He loved me, and I had faith that He could do miracles, but that was about it.

However, because I was around people who thought I was doing too much, I started to think that I was doing too much. When in reality, I wasn't doing nearly enough. We could never truly thank God enough for everything He has done for us. He is too magnificent. Instead of pursuing Christ more and growing in my relationship with God, my relationship with God remained stagnant. My friends were not necessarily on fire for God or encouraging me to grow in the things of the Lord.

My relationship with God did not begin to soar until I studied abroad in Australia. While in Australia, I visited Hope Church and got connected with a Bible study group of young Christian students. I was amazed at how many people of my age were so genuine and passionate about God and living their lives for God. That Bible study group inspired me to seek God more fervently and to deepen my relationship with Him.

I was a Christian and loved God sincerely in both of these stages of my life. However, the people in my environment influenced the depth of my walk with God. It was so much easier to grow in God when strong Christians surrounded me. When you are surrounded by people who are also pursuing sexual purity, it is easier to accomplish that goal.

You and your friends can hold each other accountable. It is good to have friends who will encourage you to stay on the right path if you are dealing with temptation or have slipped up. You can also do the same for your friends. Accountability partners are essential because moments of weakness can be liable to happen to anyone.

Accountability partners can be found within your friend group, or they can be leaders in your life. There may be someone at your church who is a mature believer and willing to be the person who holds you accountable. They can provide you with sound advice, strategies, and prayer. They can even encourage you with stories from their sexual purity journey.

If you are in a season of dating or courting, you can notify your accountability partners before you go on a date. They can pray for you and encourage you before you go out. You are less likely to succumb to temptation if you know that people are praying for you.

If you do not have any friends with the same sexual beliefs as you, pray that God sends you like-minded individuals with whom you can be friends. In the meantime, you can make good use of material on the internet that encourages a sexually pure lifestyle.

I am constantly encouraged by Christian YouTubers and bloggers who share their sexual purity journey. Their content reminds me to remain focused on my sexual purity journey. It is also good to know that you are not alone in this purity lifestyle. Other people practice sexual purity and do not succumb to sexual temptations.

Be careful when choosing mentors or people to look up to for your abstinence journey. Some people abstain from having sex with other people, but they are having sex with themselves (masturbating). Some people abstain but promote practices such as watching porn or pleasing themselves. Be sure to follow the examples of people who have a purity mindset.

Choose your romantic relationships, friendships, mentors, and accountability partners wisely. They play a bigger role than you think in your sexual purity journey. It is wise to pray and ask God to show you who you should be in romantic and platonic relationships with. I cannot express enough how much easier the sexually pure lifestyle is when like-minded people surround you.

Chapter 16:

You Are What You Consume

Whatever you put into your mind, heart, body, and spirit will come out. If you want to produce a life of sexual purity, then you need to consume pure seeds. You may think that you can cover things up and successfully hide what you are consuming because nobody sees it. However, when you are under pressure, what is in you and only what is in you will come out.

Think about a piñata. You can't expect diamonds to come out of a pinata when you only put candy in there. Under the pressure of the stick hitting the pinata, a hole is formed, and the only thing that comes out is the candy you put in there. The same thing applies to our lives.

If we fill our minds and spirits with impure movies, songs, conversations, and videos, we will act impurely in a moment of pressure because that has been instilled in us. If you do not fill your mind with pure thoughts and practical tools for remaining sexually pure, you will not have those things to draw from if you find yourself in a moment of sexual pressure.

Sometimes people fall into sexual sin because they are not prepared to live a lifestyle of purity. They may have the desire to be pure but have not thought about how they can practically achieve this goal. It is common knowledge that proper preparation creates success in many areas of our lives, like examinations in school or evaluations at work. Proper preparation will also produce success with sexual purity.

A key component in sexual purity preparation is identifying your triggers. What are some things that put you in the mood or cause you to think about having sex? The next time you have a strong urge to have sex or sexual thoughts enter your mind, think about how external sources could have possibly influenced them. It may help to write down the movies you watched, the conversations you had, the music you listened to, posts you viewed on social media, places you visited, or books you read that week.

You can take it a step further if you'd like and put these triggers up in visible spots. For example, you can create post-it notes that say, "When I watch _______, I feel _______" or "When I listen to ______, my mood changes to ______."

These visible notes can help you to remember that this struggle is present but preventable. These notes can reduce the number of times you reach for these triggers because you will remember their effects.

You may not realize it at the time, but consuming these things can affect your thoughts. I am not saying that everything you watch and listen to has to be Jesus-based 24/7. However, I want you to be aware of what you are ingesting from the things that you consume. What is the main message behind that song, movie, social media post, book, or conversation? Is that message something you want to dwell on in your spirit and mind long-term?

Similarly to how the phrase "You are what you eat" applies to the physical body, "you are what you consume" applies to your spiritual life. Your thoughts and emotions are altered based on what you watch and listen to. You may not believe me and think I am overreacting, so I have some examples.

One great example of this is seen in movies. A sad movie usually puts people in a somber mood. Sometimes they cry. A comedy normally makes people happy. People usually feel more jovial and relaxed after watching a good comedy. These are only two examples that many have experienced, but there are so many more ways that a movie can affect your mood.

When a couple is trying to have a romantic evening, they set the mood with romantic music, dim lights, alcohol, candles, etc. Things that people use to set a romantic atmosphere can be triggers for sex. These things are often done intentionally so the couple can engage in sexual intercourse.

If you are trying to abstain from sex, you should set the atmosphere for purity. Play worship music or music that does not necessarily cause you to think about sex, drink a non-alcoholic beverage, turn the lights on so you and the person you are dating can be alert, etc. The atmosphere of an environment greatly influences the activities that take place there.

This is the reason why a fine-dining restaurant has a different environment than a family entertainment restaurant. These restaurants were created for two different types of audiences. The fine-dining restaurant will have a calmer, more relaxed, elegant atmosphere because they want to attract mature adults. Family entertainment centers have an energetic and loud atmosphere because they want to attract families with children.

What is the atmosphere that you create attractively? Are you attracting sexual activity or sexual abstinence? The music we listen to, shows we watch, people we follow on social media, books we read, and the people we choose to be around can control our atmosphere. Pure atmospheres deposit purity into your soul.

Songs can be a trigger for sex as well. Some songs have foolish lyrics disguised by awesome vocals and enticing instrumentals. Listen carefully to the song lyrics. If the songs you listen to have a lot of lustful lyrics or if the artist has the spirit of lust, then you will receive a deposit of lust. The same goes for movies and the people you are around.

A friend once told me that they were struggling with sexual temptation. They were hanging out with some friends, consuming alcohol, and listening to music. Afterward, they wanted to have sex.

I asked them what type of music they were listening to. After they told me the artist's name, I asked if they thought they would be in the mood to have sex if they were listening to Christian music all night. Their response was no. Many believe that the type of music you listen to or the shows you watch do not matter, but they do. They are making deposits into you, whether you realize it or not.

If you are striving to be sexually pure, it is strongly advised that you avoid songs with sexually explicit lyrics. There are so many songs that confuse lust with love. They are called love songs, so you think they are innocent however when you listen attentively to some of them, lust is being described. This, in turn, misguides listeners about what love is. They search for love but end up in lust because they do not know any better.

So, how do you tell the difference between lust and love? I am so glad you asked! First Corinthians 13:4-8 gives a very thorough definition of love. It says, "*Love endures with patience and serenity, love is kind and thoughtful, and is not jealous or envious; love does not brag and is not proud or arrogant. It is not rude; it is not self-seeking, it is not provoked [nor overly sensitive and easily angered]; it does not take into account a wrong endured.*

It does not rejoice at injustice, but rejoices with the truth [when right and truth prevail]. Love bears all things [regardless of what comes], believes all things [looking for the best in each one], hopes all things [remaining steadfast during difficult times], endures all things [without weakening]. Love never fails [it never fades or ends]." Notice that this definition of love describes a person's character.

The definition of love in the Bible does not mention developing butterflies in your stomach, constantly thinking about someone, the chemistry between two people, eyes that sparkle, attractive bodies, good kisses, or sex. None of those things that are usually in the media or popular culture's definition of love are a part of God's definition of love.

I would like to emphasize that the Bible does not mention sex in its definition of love. So where did this notion that someone loves you because they have sex with you or want to have sex with you come from? It did not come from God. This is a perfect example of how the devil can put convincing thoughts and beliefs in your mind if you do not know the word of God.

So many people leave relationships confused because they thought they saw signs that the person loved them when all along they were seeing signs that the person was lusting after their body. Or they possibly saw signs that the person was infatuated with them. They just could not tell the difference. Some people tell someone they love them to express that they are infatuated with them.

According to the Oxford Dictionary, infatuated is an adjective that describes being "possessed with an intense but short-lived passion or admiration for someone." Signs that a person is infatuated include wanting to be around the person all the time, thinking they are perfect, constantly talking about them when you are not with them, thinking about the person all the time, being willing to do anything for the person, and feeling super happy and energetic when you are with that person. It is not unusual for people to mistake infatuation for love.

When you love someone, you see them from a more realistic viewpoint. With love, there is no clouded misjudgment that someone is perfect. You see their flaws and still choose to love them. However, infatuation and lust can be present at the same time. Sometimes you can be in so deep that you want to act upon this infatuation and lust, so you decide to be physically intimate.

You may think that you are in love and want to make love with that person.

Why is the phrase "make love" synonymous with sex? Are you truly making love when you have sex? According to First Corinthians 13:4-8, it is evident that love is made differently. Love is produced by choosing to practice patience, kindness, thoughtfulness, forgiveness, rejoicing in the truth, bearing all things, looking for the best in others, hopefulness, and endurance. Love is also made by choosing not to be jealous, envious, rude, prideful, selfish, or provoked.

God created love. As a matter of fact, First John 4:8 says, "*God IS love. [He is the originator of love, and it is an adoring attribute of His nature.]*" Similar to how a fish is a sea creature, God is love. Fundamentally, love is just a part of who He is. Does it make more sense to learn about love from the being who is love and originated it or from mere human beings who are just trying to figure it out themselves?

You may look at that definition and start to think about whether you truly show love to anyone or if someone truly shows love to you. I would like to remind you that God truly loves you! Isaiah 54:10 (NLT) says, "*For the mountains may move, and the hills disappear, but even then my faithful love for you will remain. My covenant of blessing will never be broken," says the Lord, who has mercy on you.*"

After reading this verse, if you are still struggling to believe that God truly loves you, ask Him to show you how He has proven His love to you before. God shows His love for us daily, but we sometimes don't realize it or comprehend it.

God may remind you of His remarkable example of love in the Bible, the time He sent His only son. His perfect child to earth to die on the cross for your sins. Many parents would find it hard to give up their imperfect children. However, God was thinking about you. He was being thoughtful. He knew you would need that sacrifice.

God's thoughtfulness and love show up many times in the Word of God. Psalm 139:17-18 explicitly describes God's thoughtfulness: *"How precious are your thoughts about me, O God. They cannot be numbered! I can't even count them; they outnumber the grains of sand!"* Indeed, God is extremely thoughtful if He has more thoughts than the grains of sand.

I am from The Bahamas and have spent lots of time on the beach. There is A LOT of sand on the beach. Too much to even count. Someone can spend their lifetime counting all of the grains of sand and still not finish. I implore you to explore the different facets of God's love so you can be strongly assured that He loves you.

I hope that now you begin to realize just how deep love is. Before you utter the words "I love you" again, reread First Corinthians 13:4-8 to ensure you are speaking the truth. People often tell people they love them just because it sounds good. Also, the next time someone tells you they love you, read through First Corinthians 13:4-8 to determine whether they are telling the truth. Do their actions match up with their words?

You may have to assess a relationship that you are currently in. Maybe someone has professed their love for you, and you believed it because they said it sincerely. Now you can compare their actions to the Word of God. That person may feel like they love you based on their definition of love. However, you have to decide whether you are willing to accept their profession of love based on God's definition of love.

According to the Oxford Dictionary, lust is a "strong sexual desire." You can have a strong sexual desire for someone and still love them; however, strong sexual desires should not be the only thing you have for someone. Also, that should not be the only thing someone has towards you. If you consume more popular culture than the word of God, then you are more likely to practice lust than love.

You can take this insight into the difference between love and lust and properly determine whether the music, shows, movies, and social media posts you consume are filled with lust or love. Being enlightened about the difference between love and lust also gives you more control over your life. You can make a knowledgeable decision about what you choose to let into your life.

Another sexual purity tool is to think about pure things. Philippians 4:8 says, "*...whatever is true, whatever is honorable, whatever is just, whatever is pure, whatever is lovely, whatever is commendable, if there is any excellence, if there is anything worthy of praise, think about these things.*" Be intentional with your thoughts. Thoughts may seem harmless because nobody will know them if you don't reveal them; however, they make a huge difference in our lives. Our thoughts can develop into actions.

Sometimes, impure thoughts can sneak into our minds even if we are in a pure atmosphere. However, you can get rid of those thoughts by praying, worshipping God, or choosing to think about something pure. It will feel like an awkward shift from lustful thoughts to worship thoughts, but it's worth pushing past the awkwardness. You can even rebuke the impure thought and cast it out. We should not allow impure thoughts to linger and pollute our minds.

Music is a valuable tool to help you remain pure. If you do find yourself consumed by impure thoughts or temptations, you can play worship music to shift your mindset. You can combat those impure thoughts with praise. Even if you are not in a place where you can play worship music, you can start praising God silently in your mind. Express to God how awesome and powerful you believe He is. Express your gratitude to Him for His loving kindness, grace, and faithfulness. You can even sing your favorite worship song in your mind.

We must be selective about the things we watch or see. Luke 11:34-35 says, "*Your eye is like a lamp that provides light for your body. When your eyes are healthy, your whole body is filled with light. But when it is unhealthy, your body is filled with darkness. Make sure that the light you think you have is not actually darkness.*" This scripture proves that it is important to guard what we watch.

Whatever you allow into your eye gate affects your entire body. If you constantly look at impure things, then your body will not be pure. However, your body will be pure if you constantly look at pure things. Ask the Lord to give you wisdom and discernment in the things you watch so you can be pure. Also, ask God for discipline to refrain from watching impure content.

When pursuing sexual purity, it is also beneficial to cut some things out of your life. Some places have a heavy atmosphere of lust, like dance and strip clubs, certain parties, carnival parades, and concerts. It is very advantageous not to go to these places if you are trying to be sexually pure. It is one thing to leave these types of events and not have sex afterward. However, lust has entered your mind, whether you know it or not.

James 1:14-15 says, "*But each person is tempted when they are dragged away by their own evil desire and enticed. Then, after desire has conceived, it gives birth to sin; and sin when it is full-grown, gives birth to death.*" Going to these types of social gatherings can incite lust, which causes you to be enticed to engage in sexual sin.

Sexual sin starts as a desire to have sex and leads to sex. There are already enough things that try to entice us to be sexually active, like TV commercials, internet ads, music in the gym or store, etc. You do not need to add to that enticement.

If you feel like Jesus called you to parties, clubs, and concerts to minister to people and win souls for the kingdom, I will not discourage you from doing what God told you to do. However, you should have a lifestyle of serious prayer and spending time with God through His word so the world does not end up influencing you instead of you influencing the world.

My heart desires for you to win the battle against your flesh. I want you to be victorious in your sexual purity journey. Romans 13:14 encourages us to "*Put on the Lord Jesus Christ, and make no provision for the flesh, to fulfill its lusts.*" Often, the places we go, the media we choose to absorb, and our friendships make provision for the flesh to fulfill its lusts.

Do an honest inventory of your life. Again, I urge you to reflect on where you were, who you were with, and what you were listening to or watching the last time you experienced sexual temptation. According to Romans 13:14, you need to get rid of those provisions for your flesh.

I pray that God grants you the wisdom and strength to filter what you consume and where you go. May you have heightened wisdom and discernment so you are more aware of the long-term impacts of your decisions. May God cause you to fully understand the seriousness and severity of the things you are consuming. I pray that you consume more of God, your appetite is increasing for the things of God, and He gives you a distaste for what is not like Him.

Chapter 17:

Obedience is Key

Often, the sexual purity lifestyle would be so much easier to maintain if we were being obedient to God. The Holy Spirit gives us wisdom and insight into what we should and should not do. Sometimes these things seem like they will prevent us from having fun, so we choose to be disobedient to what God told us to do. We decide that it is not that serious, and we can still be sexually pure without doing some things that God instructed us to do.

Deuteronomy 5:32 says, "*You shall be careful therefore to do as the Lord your God has commanded you. You shall not turn to the right hand or to the left.*" Sometimes, we do not do as the Lord commanded to appease our flesh. We make all sorts of left and right turns with the intention of going back to what the Lord commanded once we are done having fun.

A lot of people do not think they need to take precautions to remain pure because they believe that they are strong enough to resist temptation on their own. Sometimes, our passionate beliefs and strong desires to do something can seem like enough to help us resist temptation, but they are not. The reality is that we are human beings, and we will make mistakes. We are not perfect. Therefore, it is important to take extra precautions to resist temptation. Do not be so filled with pride that you do not take the necessary precautions to remain sexually pure.

In a marathon, side streets are usually blocked off with barricades to prevent people from taking the wrong turn. These barricades ensure that participants stay on the right track. If participants go through the wrong street, they may get lost and never end up finishing the intended course. Or, if they do manage to find their way back to the proper route, they would not get to the finish line as quickly as they could have if they stayed on the right route.

These barricades also prevent vehicles from driving on the route. This could be dangerous for the participants in the marathon. The barricades make the marathon easier for participants. They can compete without constantly watching out for vehicles or trying to figure out which street they should be taking.

Barricades can be compared to the boundaries God gives us to remain pure. If God instructs you to have boundaries in your romantic relationship, be obedient. You should not view these boundaries as brick walls caging you in and preventing you from living your best life. View them as barricades that stop you from taking the wrong turn and wasting time. Or barricades that prevent unnecessary pain from entering your life.

We have different goals that we want to accomplish and different routes to accomplish these goals. Many single Christians aim to be sexually pure and not engage in sex until marriage. However, without the proper boundaries, we can end up in the wrong romantic relationships or doing things that would affect our ability to accomplish our goals.

Some examples of boundaries that can help you remain sexually pure are refraining from kissing, cuddling, or touching and feeling each other's body inappropriately. While these things are not sex, doing these things is like pregaming for sex. When people pregame before a night out or a sports game, they usually drink alcohol and play energetic music. This puts them in that exciting party mode to have a lot of fun at a party, club, or game.

When you do things like have long passionate kissing and fondling sessions, you are prepping your body for sex. These things can ignite lust and put you in the mood for sex. Why pregame for an activity that you are not trying to do? It is better to prevent a fire than to put a fire out. This applies to sex as well. It is better to avoid a compromising situation than to get yourself out of one.

Another boundary could be not being alone in each other's house. Try to have dates in public places or around people who can hold you accountable. You may not be as strong as you think you are. This leads to another boundary: not having sleepovers with the opposite sex. Sleepovers can cause too much unnecessary temptation.

Why make your sexual purity journey even more difficult by giving yourself extra temptation? Remaining sexually abstinent has enough struggles without giving yourself the additional temptations that will arise from a sleepover. Even if you are in a long-distance relationship and your partner visits, spending money on a hotel or staying at a loved one's home is better than making yourselves vulnerable to sexual sin.

You can be creative about your dates so you can still have fun getting to know each other without isolating yourself from others. Some examples of dates in public settings include bowling, going to a skating rink, going to a carnival or an amusement park, having a picnic at a beach or park, attending a concert, having dinner or lunch at a restaurant, meeting at a coffee or ice cream shop, going to an art class, attending a cooking class, visiting museums, and hosting a game night with friends and family.

It is important to have boundaries with people you dated in the past, especially if you were sexually intimate with them. Completely relinquishing all communication or contact with your exes can also be a useful sexual purity tool. Sometimes people end a romantic relationship because God instructs them to, however, they do not entirely stop all communication with the person. They still allow that person to take up residency in their lives by calling them a "friend" instead of a boyfriend or a girlfriend.

This is dangerous because this person can still negatively influence their life and cause them to fall into sin. There is a reason why God told you to end that relationship. Also, seeing this person or continuing to communicate with this person may bring up memories in your mind about the good times the two of you had together. If you were sexually intimate, you might remember past sexual encounters and desire to experience them again.

If an opportunity presents itself, you could end up having sex with this person. This can lead to feelings of defeat and guilt. You may not understand how you could let yourself slip like that. It wasn't a slip; it was a slow fall. The fall started when you refused to completely remove that ex from your life. The fall continued when you started reminiscing about all the good times you had together. Then you hit the floor when an opportunity arose to be sexually intimate with that person.

A similar thing happened to Saul in First Samuel 15 when God instructed him to kill all of Amalek's people and animals, but he didn't follow God's instruction fully. They kept Agag (the king of Amalek) and the best sheep and cattle. God was not pleased with Saul's decision. In First Samuel 15:22-23, Samuel tells Saul, *"Obedience is better than sacrifice, and submission is better than offering the fat of rams. Rebellion is as sinful as witchcraft, and stubbornness as bad as worshipping idols. So, because you have rejected the command of the Lord, he has rejected you as king."*

Saul's partial obedience cost him his position as king. This passage of scripture teaches a strong lesson in obedience. When God tells us to do something, we should carry out those instructions fully. God may be withholding things from you now because of your disobedience. Partial obedience is disobedience. If you feel like God is telling you to end relationships, end them completely. God is all-knowing, so He knows what is best for you.

Use discernment in this area. If you have to be around your ex in a public setting like a church, work, or school, then you should still be cordial and respectful towards them. Also, if you have children with your ex, you should still be in communication for the children's sake. Don't prevent your children from seeing their other parent because you want to move on. This can have a serious negative impact on your children.

Another useful sexual purity boundary can be refraining from masturbation. Many people use masturbation as a mechanism to help them remain abstinent. However, during this time of singleness, you should focus on God and depend on Him to help you fight temptation. You should draw closer to God as you strive to remain sexually pure. When you masturbate to satisfy your sexual desires, you remove God from the equation and insert yourself to meet your needs.

Masturbation could be classified as idolatry because you depend on yourself to remain abstinent until marriage instead of God. Your season of abstinence is meant to bring you closer to God and rely on Him more. You should pray to God and seek His help when tempted. Also, you are not becoming more disciplined and overcoming that sexual urge. You are feeding into it by taking matters into your own hands and pleasing yourself.

By masturbating when you have sexual urges, you are simply fanning the fire instead of putting it out. You are still satisfying the urge instead of starving it. You ultimately give in to your sexual urges instead of telling your body that you don't need them. The more you build up discipline and continue to deny your body the immediate pleasure of satisfying that urge, the less you will have that urge. It may come back from time to time because it is a natural human desire, but not as frequent or intense.

Masturbation is like cheating on a quiz from someone with the wrong answers. You end up not passing the quiz, and you miss an opportunity to learn valuable things that can positively impact your life. When someone does not prepare properly for a quiz, any answer can seem like the correct answer. There's a desperation to succeed despite preparation, so anything that can be written down will work.

When you have not properly thought out your plan for being sexually pure, masturbation can seem like a great solution. However, it is not a good solution. Pastor Tim Ross gave a beautiful analogy of masturbation in a video I watched. He compared masturbation to getting stuffed with four peanut butter and jelly sandwiches before going to a restaurant to eat a delicious meal. By the time you get to the restaurant, you'll be full because you've eaten four sandwiches already.

When people anticipate a nice, elevated, out-of-the-ordinary dining experience, they often save their appetites because they want to have enough space in their stomachs to eat all the nice food. They don't want to miss out on anything because they are full.

Sex within marriage can be compared to that elevated dining experience. You will cheapen that experience by masturbating because you are pleasing your flesh with something that is not as good as the full sexual experience. There are so many things that a person who loves and cares for you can provide that masturbation could never give. Imagine missing out on the amazing pleasures of sex within marriage just because you're sexually full.

Trust God with your urges. Give them to Him. Ask Him to help you on the journey of sexual purity. Rely on His strength. Let Him be your sufficiency. It may be useful to play worship music when you get a desire to have sex or masturbate. By choosing to worship God instead of masturbating, you break the desire to worship yourself by worshipping the Creator. Exercising is also a healthy tool to help you release energy when you are experiencing sexual urges.

Psalm 119:9 says, *"How can a young person stay pure? By obeying your word."* The Bible gives the best tips for sexual purity. Remaining pure is easier when we obey God's commandments in His word. Many people cherry-pick the commandments that they want to obey from the Bible. This leads to an inconsistent and impure lifestyle. What are your standards based on, if not the word of God? Study God's word and ask Him to help you to obey ALL of the commandments of the Bible. James 4:17 tells us, *"Whoever knows the right thing to do and fails to do it, for him it is a sin."*

We are fortunate that God graciously forgives us of our sins if we repent. There are many scriptures in the Bible that confirm this. Acts 3:19 says, *"Repent, then, and turn to God, so that your sins may be wiped out, that times of refreshing may come from the Lord."* This is great news! There is no need to wallow in guilt and shame. Once you go to God and repent, He will forgive you and clean your record. He will restore and empower you.

Repentance is another key component to remaining sexually pure. People often repent of sexual sin after the relationship ends. The main reason behind their repentance is their desire to relinquish their feelings for their previous partner. They want to move on but are unable to do so because they maintain a connection (soul tie) with their ex.

They think that if they repent, they will finally be able to move on. However, this type of repentance is not genuine. You should repent because you want to be in the right standing with God. The Oxford Dictionary defines repent as "feel or express sincere regret or remorse about one's wrongdoing or sin." If you are only repenting to rid yourself of feelings you have for a former partner, then you do not truly feel remorse about your sin. Chances are, if you got into another relationship, you would engage in premarital sex with that person as well.

Your repentance should be about building your relationship with God. You should be seeking to get closer to God by repenting, not closer to your next romantic relationship. You should not take God's grace and mercy for granted. Many people continuously fall into sexual sin because they know God is gracious. They can ask Him for forgiveness.

By taking God's grace for granted, you trivialize the blood that Christ shed on the cross. Second Corinthians 6:1 says, "*We then, as workers together with Him also plead with you not to receive the grace of God in vain.*" Jesus Christ endured the ultimate sacrifice by dying on the cross for our sins. Don't trivialize this supernatural act of love by deliberately sinning, because you know that God will extend His grace towards you and forgive you.

When we continue to take God's grace for granted, our hearts become hardened toward God. Romans 2:5 says, "*But because you are stubborn and refuse to turn from your sin, you are storing up terrible punishment for yourself.*" When you continuously ask God for forgiveness and still repeat the same sin pattern, you are not truly turning from your sin. You are not fooling God one bit. He knows exactly what you are doing and where your heart is.

People often say, "Only God can judge me," as though this gives them the freedom to do whatever they want. However, it is quite the contrary. This is a profoundly serious statement. Only God truly knows your heart. He can judge whether you are being sincere. According to Romans 2:6, when judgment day comes, "*He will render to each one according to his works.*"

Do not allow your desire to fill a void to cause you to face harsh consequences on judgment day. The truth is, you are looking to have a void filled in relationships. However, God can fill those voids much better than a relationship. He has filled voids for so many people before, including me. It is such a fantastic feeling! I know He can do the same for you.

John 4 tells the story of Jesus meeting a woman at a well who had been involved with multiple men throughout her life and was in an adulterous relationship at the time. The woman went to the well for water, but He knew she needed so much more. Jesus told her, *"Whoever drinks of the water that I will give him will never be thirsty again. The water I will give him will become in him a spring of water welling up to eternal life"* (John 4:14).

I am sure this woman's life was changed forever after her encounter with Jesus. Your life can change as well. You, too, can partake of the living water that God provides. Just ask Him to fill you with His living water and believe it is done. After drinking the living water, you will truly understand that nothing can fill the voids that God can.

When you repent sincerely, you should ask God to deliver you from your sexual sins and make you whole. Only God can truly make you whole. He is the only one who can fill those voids in your heart. Once Christ has made you whole, you would not desire a relationship just to fill your voids and give you some false sense of security.

Another tool for remaining sexually pure is finding things to occupy your time. People tend to fall into sin when they have a lot of idle time. The less idle time you have, the less time you have to be tempted. There is nothing wrong with having some free time throughout the day to relax and do leisurely activities like reading or watching a movie. However, danger can arise when you constantly have free time. When this happens, you can become bored, and since your mind is unoccupied, the enemy can begin to put the wrong thoughts and ideas into your mind.

Ephesians 5:15-16 says, *"Look carefully then how you walk, not as unwise but as wise, making the best use of the time, because the days are evil."* If you have a lot of free time, there are so many things you can do to occupy yourself. For instance, you can serve in a ministry at your church, join a service group, learn new skills by participating in classes or sessions online (there are a lot of websites that offer free classes or webinars), or spend more time in God's word so you can be spiritually strong.

You can even offer to babysit children so parents can go on a date night or have a break. A lot of single parents rarely have a break from their children, and they may not be able to afford a babysitter. Offering to babysit so they can go out and have adult fun or get much-needed rest can be a tremendous blessing.

You can also use this time to build your prayer life. There is never a shortage of things to pray for. Everyone needs prayers, no matter how rich and successful they may seem. If you happen to run out of people or things to pray for, you can just listen to the news, and your prayer list will certainly grow. I can't tell you how many times listening to the news led to me praying for people in countries that I've never visited or even heard of.

Reading the Bible is also a good way to build up your prayer life. You can pray different scriptures over your life and the lives of your loved ones. As you learn more about God through His word, you will also have a deeper connection to Him, and praying will seem second nature to you.

I only listed a few suggestions; however, you can do many other things if you have time, such as mentoring others, volunteering at an orphanage or retirement home, or learning a new sport. Praying to God and asking Him what He wants you to do with your time is important. He created you for a special purpose. He would be the best person to tell you what you should be doing with your skillset. Ephesians 5:17 says, "*Therefore do not be foolish, but understand what the will of the Lord is.*"

When you obey what God tells you to do, you will find yourself walking in your purpose and living a more fulfilled life. You will experience fewer temptations because you will be preoccupied with doing the kingdom's work. There is so much to be done for the kingdom of God. However, more people are needed to accomplish these things. Matthew 9:37 says, *"The harvest truly is plentiful, but the laborers are few."*

The devil wants to distract us so there will be fewer people to do the work of the Lord and win souls for Christ. Do not become distracted. Commit your time to the Lord so more people can be a part of the kingdom of God. Many people are struggling, and you could be the person who connects them to God so they are set free and have a more abundant life.

This book is a direct result of my asking God what He wants me to do with my time. He instructed me to write a book about sexual purity. If I had never inquired of God, I would not have written this book. I am not a traditional author. I have a Chemistry degree. In college, I was encouraged to write as little as possible. I was taught how to write chemical formulas, so I do not have to use as many words.

Never in my wildest dreams did I ever think I would be writing a book. I love God deeply and want to fulfill His purpose for my life on this earth. Since that includes writing a book, I did that. Honestly, I have been enjoying this writing journey. I feel so connected to God and full of peace and joy when I write. You may find a new passion or hobby after submitting your time to God and being obedient to what He tells you to do. Submit your time to God so that He may receive the glory.

I pray that you feel encouraged to comply with the boundaries God has instructed you to have in your life. May God lead and guide you so that you have success in your purity journey. I pray that you use this time of singleness to become all that God wants you to be. May you become more obedient and sensitive to the voice of the Lord. I pray that you allow the Lord to consume your time and thoughts, so there is no room for the enemy to infiltrate. May the Lord grant you peace, wisdom, and rest in Him as you grow into all He wants you to be. In Jesus Christ's name, I pray, Amen.

Chapter 18:

Count the Cost!
(Unpleasant Results of Remaining Pure)

Taking the time to "count the cost" will prevent you from easily giving up on your sexual purity journey. I will admit that I have contemplated whether remaining sexually pure was worth it after realizing the cost. However, with the help of God, I concluded that it was SOOO worth it. In Luke 14:25–33, Jesus implores people to count the cost of following Him. He says, *"Whoever does not bear his own cross and come after me cannot be my disciple"* (Luke 14:27).

The "cross" in this verse can be symbolic. It symbolizes the inconvenience and hardship we would have to endure to follow God. Sometimes God requires us to do difficult things with unfavorable consequences. However, as His followers, we are required to do these things anyway. These things make us better people and help us advance God's kingdom.

Jesus further explains His statement with an example. He says, *"For which of you, desiring to build a tower, does not first sit down and count the cost, whether he has enough to complete it? Otherwise, when he has laid a foundation and is not able to finish, all who see it begin to mock him, saying, 'This man began to build and was not able to finish'"* (Luke 14:28-30).

I think this happens to Christians sometimes. We have great intentions to do things for the Lord; however, after initiating the process and being met with unfavorable outcomes, we quit. We did not count the cost before starting the venture. Having a sexually pure lifestyle can have unexpected repercussions other than sexual urges you cannot act on.

In this section, I want to share some ways that being sexually pure can cost you, so you can be better prepared when these things come up. I am not writing this chapter to deter you from the sexual purity lifestyle. However, I want you to be aware of these things in case they arise, so you will not be caught off guard. You would be fully aware of what is going on and be better equipped to resist the temptation to be sexually active.

Rejection is a cross that sexually abstinent people must endure. Sometimes, people reject what they don't understand. In some instances, the rejection is intentional, other times, it is not. To many people, fornication is normal. They do it, and all their friends and family do it too. They think it is weird for people to refrain from having sex. Also, many people have never even met someone who is practicing sexual abstinence.

I remember the first time I received a form of rejection for being a virgin. My very own mother excluded me. I was still in high school and was at a family friend's house. Someone younger than me mentioned that they were no longer virgins and were talking a little bit about their sexual history. My mother told me that I had to leave the room where all the adults were and go into the room where the little children played video games. This felt like a social demotion.

They were going to talk about sex, and although I was older, she did not want me to be in the room because I was a virgin. I have since gotten over it, but I was pretty hurt at the time. I was the only person who had to leave the room awkwardly. I was also a bit offended because I had the same qualifications as a Bahamian high school graduate at that point. This happened during the summer before my senior year of high school, and I had already passed all the exams that twelfth graders in The Bahamas are required to take (Bahamas General Certificate of Secondary Education examinations).

I took these examinations a year early. I thought I was as smart as any grown person in society. Virginity felt like an inconvenience at that point. I thought of people I could have sex with so I would no longer be treated like an innocent little girl. However, I could not think of anyone worth losing my virginity to. Losing my virginity was always a big deal, and I wanted to do it with someone special. I did not want to have regrets about that later in life.

Another form of rejection that sexually abstinent people can experience is from potential mates. Some people still think it's weird to be a virgin at a certain age. People can lose interest in having a romantic relationship with someone after finding out that they are not sexually active. Some people also want to have a relationship with someone they can have sex with regularly. This is normal for them. They are not willing to be sexually abstinent, so they choose not to date people who are.

You might meet an attractive person who you have chemistry with; they are levelheaded, successful, goal-oriented, mannerly, and love the Lord, however, you find out that they are not willing to be sexually abstinent. That could be very disappointing. You may even start thinking about whether sex is a big deal. I know it may seem like you are giving up a good thing that you may never find again. I am single, so I know how rare it is to meet someone who has a lot of the qualities you are looking for in a mate.

However, you must believe that you do not have to compromise your standards or beliefs for the person whom God has for you. If you find yourself in a position where you have to compromise your purity standards, then that person is not who God has for you, or you are not supposed to be together in this season. Staying with that person can delay the time in which your God-ordained life partner comes along.

Society at large typically rejects sexually abstinent people. I can't tell you how many times I've heard a negative comment in a public setting about someone who is practicing sexual abstinence. There are also several movies and television shows where people make derogatory remarks about virgins or people who are sexually abstinent. This can create fear in your mind. You may begin to think that you will never meet someone with the same purity goals as you.

Therefore, it is so important to guard what you consume. If that social circle, television show, song, book, podcast, etc., makes you feel less valuable because you are choosing to abstain from sex until marriage, then stop spending time on those things. There is Christian content that you can consume instead that can be just as entertaining. Throughout my life, I received a lot of encouragement from Christian friends, YouTubers, bloggers, and songwriters to stay pure.

Stories about abstinent Christians who met spouses with the same spiritual convictions encourage me. These Christian examples help defeat the myth that there is nobody willing to wait to have sex until marriage. I have also found that there are several Christian men and women in their late twenties and thirties who are virgins. There are more people practicing self-control than you think. Don't let the enemy fool you into thinking you and your two Christian friends are the only abstinent people on earth, so you will have to compromise in that area if you don't want to be single for the rest of your life.

I would just like to encourage you not to allow rejection to instill fear and doubt within you. Continue to be obedient and faithful to God despite what others have to say or how they treat you. Your purity testimony can be the very thing that inspires someone else, and they can inspire others. You can create a continuous wave of people being encouraged to remain sexually pure. Don't end the wave before you even start it.

First Peter 2:4 says you may be *"a living stone rejected by men but in the sight of God [you are] chosen and precious."* This verse just makes my heart glad. It is beautiful, honorable, and humbling to be considered chosen and precious by the King of kings. I live for the one who calls me chosen and precious, not merely human beings, so I will strive to please Him in all I do.

I believe that many people who choose to be sexually abstinent are rejected because they are misunderstood. Often, people are perceived as being homosexual or boring if they choose not to be sexually active during their single season. It is common for males to be perceived as soft or less masculine if they are not sexually active. This can be challenging and lead to a desire to prove themselves. It is also hurtful and emotionally taxing when people say things about you that are not true. This is, unfortunately, another cross that Christian singles must bear.

When people find out you are a virgin, they tend to treat you like you are green (naïve or innocent), which can sometimes feel degrading. This can be a bad feeling, especially since being green is not generally considered a good thing. However, I am quite happy and proud to be green in the area of sex. It was not God's intention for us to experience sex before marriage, so being green in this area means I am walking in God's will for my life.

Just because I accepted this truth does not mean that others have. I have experienced my virginity being made fun of. People thought it was appropriate to joke about it or call me names like "Virgin Mary." I had to develop a thick skin and a strong belief that people's opinions do not matter in my life. In those moments, I remind myself why I chose to wait until marriage to have sex. Although I get offended by people who make a mockery of my sacrifice to the Lord, I choose not to dwell on it.

The fear of missing out can also be a big determining factor in people's sexual purity journeys. Some virgins may fear missing out on the sexual experience that so many people brag about.

They want to be an active participant in conversations about sex instead of being excluded from the conversation. They do not want to miss out on having sex before getting married, so they decide to try it. People can also fear missing out on being in a romantic relationship. They may settle for someone who they have to sleep with to please so that they are not lonely.

Non-virgins who decide to abstain from sex have their cross to bear as well. People often make snarky comments or jokes about those who are sexually abstinent in general. Many people think it is tyrannical for someone to decide not to have sex outside of marriage after they have already done it. They think that the person should just continue to have sex. They don't see the point in stopping something that you enjoy. There is a unique mindset that says if you have already slipped up, you should just continue.

Sexual purity is important despite sexual history. As long as you breathe, it is never too late to get on the right track with the Lord. God does not look at your sexual past as a reason to ignore the recent effort you have put into being sexually pure. When God forgives us, He gives us a clean slate. In Isaiah 43:25, God says, *"I—yes, I alone—will blot out your sins for my own sake and will never think of them again."* If God forgets about your sins, then you do not have a reason to hold on to them and use them as a crutch not to move on and improve your life.

Don't let people who try to negate your sexual purity efforts cause you to fall off track. It is obvious that they do not know the Bible, so why take spiritual advice from them? With God's help, you can have a sexually pure lifestyle despite your sexual history. God will honor your diligence and sacrifice. Once you repent and ask for forgiveness, God will not keep a record of your wrongdoings. He shows you that it is possible to start over with a clean slate.

Last but certainly not least, the greatest cross that single Christians have to bear regarding sexual purity is the urge to have sex. People who have previously had sex may struggle more with sexual urges than virgins. It's like craving ice cream. If you have never tasted ice cream before but have just seen it and heard people describe it, then your desire for ice cream will not be as strong as someone who has experienced it before or someone who has experienced multiple flavors.

Yes, virgins have sexual urges however, in most cases, it is not as intense as those of people who have experienced sex before and enjoyed it. Do not allow those urges to cause you to give in to sexual temptation. A good way to overcome these urges is to have a plan in place or a list of things you can do when you have sexual urges. Pray, take a cold shower, exercise, listen to worship music or something inspirational, have a trusted friend who you can call who can encourage you not to fall into sexual sin, etc.

Sometimes you can be around a person who can trigger your sexual urges. You may be drawn to the way they look, the scent of their perfume or cologne, the way they walk, and their smile, and if they hug you, you may feel as if you could melt. It can be hard to even focus on them. They can be talking, and you seem to be paying attention, but your mind is elsewhere. Sometimes you get fogged-brained from the excitement of seeing them, and you forget all about your purity goals.

A good strategy for situations like this is to whisper a prayer. It doesn't have to be long. If you know you're about to see this person, you can just pray a simple "Lord help me" prayer. The length of the prayer could be adjusted based on the amount of time you have before your interaction. Sometimes you may unexpectedly run into this person and must quickly say this prayer within the first few seconds of your interaction before your mind drifts off. God will help you.

Psalm 46:1 (NKJV) says, "*God is our refuge and strength, A very present help in trouble.*" Sometimes we do not receive God's help amid difficult situations because we do not ask Him for it. Don't be too embarrassed or ashamed to ask God for help with your sexual urges. He already knew about them anyway. He wants to help you accomplish sexual purity.

Some people have sexual partners who are always willing and ready to have sex with them whenever they reach out. If there is a person, you can contact or have contacted in the past who will help you to give in to that urge, block and delete that person on your phone and every social media account. You may even need to change your number in case they try to contact you.

You do not need to have an emergency backup plan to sin. If you are in a romantic relationship with someone, it is important to set boundaries in your relationship. Boundaries can help you defeat moments of weakness when you have sexual urges.

I desired to heighten your awareness of the negative aspects of sexual purity. I hope you are more vigilant and aware of the enemy's tactics to lure you away from the sexual purity lifestyle. I pray that you please God with your life. I also pray that your sexual purity journey is so successful that you set great examples of the sexual purity lifestyle for others to follow.

Chapter 19:

God Has Everything You Need

Several years ago, I attended a church service where I heard a song that made me reflect on my views about the sufficiency of God. I started to sing along with the praise team but stopped when I realized that I did not think Christ was truly all that I needed. At that point in my life, Christ was not enough because I wanted other things that I thought would add satisfaction to my life. I had yet even begun to comprehend the fullness of Christ.

My views about Christ began to evolve when I heard the remainder of the song's lyrics. The song expressed how God has everything we could ever possibly want and need. I paused and thought about the lyrics, then realized that they were true. Christ is truly all I require because He is capable of providing for me. Christ truly has EVERYTHING that I need. Philippians 4:19 says, *"And my God shall supply all your need according to His riches in glory by Christ Jesus."* If we genuinely believed that verse, we would not try to get our needs met from so many other sources.

Some people choose not to be sexually pure because they are relying on a mere human to meet their needs. They need their bills paid, groceries, or the latest electronics and clothes. They exchange these items for sex instead of relying on God to supply their needs. God does not always provide at the exact second we want Him to, but He ALWAYS provides on time.

It is in God's nature to provide for His children. God is Jehovah-Jireh. This means He is the God who provides. Genesis 22 gives a great example of God providing when you remain steadfast and faithful to Him. In Genesis 22, God instructs Abraham to offer his son as a burnt offering.

Abraham was obedient and took his son to be offered as a burnt offering. God sent an angel to stop him at the very last moment after Abraham had already bound his son, laid him on the altar, and was about to slay him with a knife. Then Abraham saw a ram caught in a thicket. He offered the ram up for a burnt offering instead of his son. This situation proved that Abraham feared God.

God wants to deliver many people, but they have not given God a chance. They do not wait long enough to get the opportunity to witness God being their provider. For instance, instead of waiting for God to bless them with Christian companionship, many Christians hang around with worldly people who will only distract them and lead them astray.

Instead of waiting for God to provide for them financially, many people go to other people, number houses to gamble the little money that they do have or steal the money. Instead of going to God to find out His plans for their future, many people go to fortune tellers or psychics. Some people even go to witches or warlocks who can give them potions to use to make things happen in their lives instead of just waiting for God's will to be done.

Before you start thinking I am crazy for mentioning witches and warlocks, I just want to point out that they are not fictional characters solely created for entertainment in books and movies. They are real. The Bible mentions them in scripture verses such as Second Chronicles 33:6, Leviticus 19:31, Revelation 18:23, Galatians 5:19-20, and Isaiah 47:8-14.

Often, Christians do not take full advantage of the stress relief that God provides. Instead of relying on God to be their stress reliever, they use sex, weed, alcohol, or drugs to help them cope with their stress. These other sources are simply distractions. They ultimately distract Christians from having a true relationship with Christ.

People are distracted by things like sex, weed, societal status, money/gambling, partying, and alcohol. Psalms 1:1-3 says, "*Oh, the joys of those who do not follow the advice of the wicked, or stand around with sinners, or join in with mockers. But they delight in the law of the Lord, meditating on it day and night. They are like trees planted along the riverbank, bearing fruit each season. Their leaves never wither, and they prosper in all they do.*"

The blessings of sticking with God far outweigh the temporary satisfaction of engaging in sin. Although many profess Christianity or say they believe in God, Christ is not enough for them. They have not realized that Christ can provide anything they could need and more. Some people do not stick it out long enough with Christ to experience Him being their provider.

God loves us genuinely. Sometimes He makes us wait because He wants us to grow while we are waiting. He is developing us during the waiting process. Habakkuk 2:3 says, "*If it seems slow in coming, wait. It's on its way. It will come right on time.*" God is all-knowing, so He knows the right time to bless you. He wants you to be equipped to handle the blessing when it comes.

There was a deeper level of intimacy Abraham experienced with God after He provided the ram in the thicket. He truly experienced Jehovah-Jireh. God has given me miraculous provisions on multiple occasions. Each provision caused me to trust God more and cling closer to Him. As a result, my relationship with God improved. It was no longer a surface-level relationship.

I no longer see God as this distant being in the heavens that I must obey if I do not want to go to hell. I felt closer to God. I began to spend more time with Him because I went to Him with my needs more often. I had confidence that He would provide for me, and He did.

God has provided for me financially on numerous occasions, such as when I was in college, and I studied abroad in Australia for several months. When I left The Bahamas, my funds were limited. I only had enough money for a one-way ticket (yes, I did not know how I was going to pay for my ticket to return home), a few months of rent (it was not enough for the entire semester), a phone, and some change to purchase food on a strict budget.

Anyone who has ever visited Australia can tell you that it is not a cheap place to live. I went into a store that sold one bottle of Gatorade for five Australian dollars. There was a restaurant that sold hamburgers for 20 Australian dollars each, and they did not come with any sides.

I was fully aware of the fact that Australia had a high cost of living before traveling there, and I still decided to walk out on faith and live there with my limited budget. This might sound untrue, but some of the staff in the bursar's office laughed at me when my university's Office of International Education informed them that I planned to study abroad in Australia. They knew I could not afford it and mocked me, but they still approved my application to study abroad.

Can I tell you that God blessed me more than I expected while in Australia? I was only praying for Him to meet my needs, but He did more than that. He gave me money to buy my plane ticket back home, eat out frequently, visit cool places like the Great Barrier Reef, see Lion King live at the theater, buy souvenirs for my friends and family, and even treat a friend to dinner to thank her for being so kind to me during my time in Australia.

This is only one story of how God blessed my life. I have so many more testimonies of His undeserving goodness and grace toward me. Do not give up on God. Stick in there. I can guarantee that He will provide for you.

God is the well that never runs dry. He can continually supply our needs, and He enjoys doing it. In John 4:14, Jesus says, *"Everyone who drinks this water will get thirsty again and again.*

Anyone who drinks the water I give will never thirst—not ever. The water I give will be an artesian spring within, gushing fountains of endless life."

The satisfaction that the world gives will not quench your thirst forever. For instance, if you use sex to quench your thirst for stress relief and companionship, you will have to quench your thirst constantly. That good feeling from a sexual encounter does not last forever. However, if we go to God to quench our thirst, we will never be thirsty again.

Who or what has been quenching your thirst? Who have you been going to so your needs can be met? Do these people/things make you fully satisfied? I implore you to go to God the next time you have a need. Allow Him to make you whole. Allow Him to supply your needs. Ask God to forgive you for your sins in your attempt to supply your needs without Him.

"Wait patiently for the Lord. Be brave and courageous. Yes, wait patiently for the Lord" (Psalm 27:14). You may make a mistake and give in the first few times you try to wait on the Lord, but my prayer is that you do not give up. I pray you do not lose hope and keep trying until you get it right. Keep trying until you see a breakthrough in your life. I pray that you allow God to be Jehovah-Jireh to you and that you see the manifestation of His goodness in your life.

Chapter 20:

Encouragement

You did not pick up this book and read to this point by happenstance. I believe that God had you in mind when He instructed me to write this book. He knew that this resource would edify, encourage, and empower you. Freedom from past sexual sins is your portion. If I can obtain sexual purity, then you can too. It is not impossible. May I repeat, IT IS NOT IMPOSSIBLE.

Many single people speak word curses over their lives by saying things like, "I just can't go a long period without having sex." Some people think they need sex to let go of tension. They feel that if they do not have sex, they will be tense and miserable all the time. I want to let you know that these popular sayings and thoughts are false.

In Matthew 19:26, Jesus tells His disciples, *"With God all things are possible."* This means, with God's help, it is possible to abstain from sex for a long time, no matter how much you enjoy it. It is also possible for you to not have sex and not be tense and miserable all the time. Sex can have good effects on the body, but other practices can achieve similar effects, such as releasing tension as well.

Some of you may feel it's too late to be sexually pure because you have already lost your virginity. It is not too late, and God can still use you. The Bible has many stories of people who made sinful choices, and God redeemed them. For instance, Genesis 16 reveals the story of Abram impregnating his wife's maidservant. He did this because he and his wife were growing impatient and less hopeful about having a child. However, in James 2:23,

Abraham is still referred to as "the friend of God" despite his mistakes.

Second Samuel 11 tells the story of how David got Bathsheba pregnant and had her husband killed. However, God forgave David for these egregious acts. He still had to deal with the consequences of his actions, although he was forgiven. God allowed David and Bathsheba's baby to die (Second Samuel 12:13-14,18). However, in Acts 13:22, God refers to him as "a man after My own heart." He knew the mistakes David would make even before he made them, but He still considered David to be a man after His own heart. That is why it is so powerful.

Both Abram and David are examples in the Bible of people who committed sexual sins, but God forgave them. God allowed them to turn their lives around, and that same opportunity is available for you. One of my favorite stories in the Bible of someone who strayed away and acted irresponsibly but received redemption is the story of the prodigal son.

The story of the prodigal son can be found in Luke 15:11–32. I like this parable because it reveals God's ability to show us compassion and forgiveness. In this parable, a man asks his father for his inheritance and then squanders it. After he had spent all his inheritance, he was in need, so he got a job where he fed pigs. He realized that his father's servants were living better than him, so he decided to return home to work for his father.

When he returned home, his father was so happy that he gave him royal treatment and had a celebration for him. His father did not treat him the way his son thought he would. One part of this story that stood out to me is Luke 15:18-19. These verses reveal that the prodigal son got to a place where he understood the severity of his actions and truly regretted his decisions.

As he rehearses what he will say to his father, he says, "*Father, I have sinned against heaven and before you, and I am no longer worthy to be called your son. Make me like one of your hired servants*" (Luke

15:18-19 NKJV). He got to the point where he had a repentant heart.

You have to get to the point where you genuinely regret straying from God, and you will return to Him because you realize life is truly better with God.

Just like God, the prodigal son's father celebrated him, although he did not deserve it. God rejoices in your genuine repentance and returns to Him. You are a celebrated individual. Like the prodigal son's father, God celebrates your return. When your return is celebrated, it's a special thing.

The prodigal son did not slip in through the backdoor and hide behind the scenes where nobody noticed him. No, a celebration was held in his honor because he was loved and valued by his father. His father considered him to be special. That celebration would motivate anybody to remain on the right path.

I think the celebration and the way the father treated his son like royalty when he returned are such an important part of this story. When you feel valued in a place, it is difficult to leave easily. This is why so many companies and organizations invest in making their staff feel valued and appreciated. They know this will influence their staff to stick with their company for the long haul and even put in the extra effort to perform their tasks with excellence.

What often happens is that people stray from God, and when they return, they believe the lies the enemy tells them about how useless they are or how God does not see any value in them. To add to that dilemma, some churches treat Christians who have strayed very poorly once they return. They look down on them and lead them to believe that the only place they belong in the church is in the back pew.

Many people in this circumstance end up straying away from God again because the world shows them more love and acceptance than the church. Also, they created this narrative in their mind that they are not valuable to God or that God can't use them. If you have ever strayed from God or if you have a strained relationship with God now, I want you to know that God still loves and values you tremendously. It is not too late to repent and turn back to God.

There are no perfect Christians, so there is no reason for you to feel less than anyone else. Romans 3:23-24 says, *"For all have sinned and fall short of the glory of God, and are justified by his grace as a gift, through the redemption that is in Christ Jesus."* Once you have realized that your past sinful actions do not disqualify you from being seen as valuable and loved by God, you can work on building your confidence in the fact that you can overcome your past sins.

Some people believe that they should continue to sin because they are already on the path of premarital sex. They think there is no going back. But there is renewal, restoration, and hope in God's forgiveness. Micah 7:19 informs us that *"[God] will have compassion on us. [God] will trample our sins under [His] feet and throw them into the depths of the ocean!"* (Micah 7:19 NLT). God has forgotten about your past. Why allow that to hold you back?

It is important to remember Philippians 4:13, which says, *"I can do all things through Christ who strengthens me."* Believe that this is true in your life. You can overcome past sexual sins with God's help. Your future can be different from your past. It may be difficult to be sexually pure, but it is not impossible. Anything is possible with God's help. I could not be sexually pure on my own. I need God's help with sexual purity, like in every other area of my life. You could obtain purity in EVERY area of your life with God's help!

Just because you have made up your mind that you will turn away from past sins and live your life to please God, does not mean you will not be tempted anymore. James 1:12 says, *"Blessed is the man who endures temptation; for when he has been approved, he will receive the crown of life which the Lord has promised to those who love Him."*

This verse lets us know that we will be tempted. I want you to know that you will be tempted, but the information I have provided in this book can help you to be prepared when temptation arises. Have your strategies in place so you can resist temptation each time it pops up. Go get your "crown of life" that the Lord has promised. Christ died on the cross, so you don't have to be in bondage to any sin pattern.

God ensures that He will help us resist temptation in His word. First Corinthians 10:13 says, *"No temptation has overtaken you that is not common to man. God is faithful, and he will not let you be tempted beyond your ability, but with the temptation, he will also provide the way of escape, that you may be able to endure it."* The next time you are tempted, remember that the fight is fixed in your favor.

God said in His word that He would not allow you to "be tempted beyond your ability." The fight against temptation is fixed to suit your capabilities. You can face that temptation with the confidence that you can overcome it. Sometimes we give up and don't even try to resist the temptation because we don't think we are strong enough to resist it. Our mindset must change to that of an overcomer.

First Corinthians 10:13 also points out that God will *"provide the way of escape."* The next time you are tempted, ask God to reveal the way of escape to you. Have the mindset and will to escape, so you do not fall into temptation. God provides us with ways to escape temptation, however, we sometimes do not see the escape, or we do not feel like escaping. After all, if we are not being lured in by something that entices us, it would not be a temptation.

Whatever we are being tempted with can seem better than an escape, so we choose not to escape. Before your next temptation arises, you can pray and ask God to help you to see the way of escape and give you the discipline to choose to escape. You can ask God to help you resist temptation before your next temptation even arises. This is one of the beautiful things about reading scripture. You can learn about God's promises and pray more effectively.

According to the Bible, Christ is our advocate. First John 2:1 says, "*If anyone does sin, we have an advocate who pleads our case before the Father. He is Jesus Christ, the one who is truly righteous.*" Jesus could have chosen not to have anything to do with us, but He chose to be an advocate for us. I am quite sure that some of you would not advocate for people if you truly knew their flaws.

If you knew someone who had a problem with being untruthful, you probably would not advocate for them because you would not know whether they could be trusted. However, Christ sees us in our sins, knows when we will sin again, and still advocates for us. That is perfect, unexplainable, incomprehensible love.

Yes, you may have messed up in the past, but you do not have to worry about that because the best lawyer ever is advocating for you! It is not too late for you to start over, and it is not impossible to endure the path of purity. The Creator of the universe is on your side, rooting for you!! I am so grateful that Christ is our advocate!

One great story in the Bible that clearly shows how our past does not matter once we give our lives to Christ and ask for God's forgiveness is the parable of the workers in the vineyard in Matthew 20:1-16. In this parable, a man goes out early in the morning to hire laborers for his vineyard. He agreed with the laborers to pay them one denarius per day to work in his vineyard. As the day progressed, he hired more people to work in his vineyard.

At the end of the day, the vineyard owner paid everyone the same wage. The people who started working at the eleventh hour received the same compensation as the people who started working that morning.

This parable compares the owner of the vineyard to God. God finds people who are willing to work for Him here on earth. However, it does not matter whether the person got saved and began working for God at a young age or an old age. When Christians die, they go to heaven irrespective of how long they have been saved and how much work they have done for the kingdom of God.

Someone could give their life to Christ and die one hour later. That person would still go to heaven. I shared this parable to encourage anyone who thinks it is too late for them to turn their life around. It is not too late. You can still commit your life to Christ and decide to work to advance His kingdom here on earth. You would be just as eligible to spend eternity in heaven as someone who committed their life to Christ as a child.

Just think about the person in the parable who started working at the eleventh hour. If that person decided to stay home and not work because it was late, they would not have received that generous payment for their work. Do not miss out on your heavenly reward because you think it's too late. It is not too late to fully commit your life to God and have a lifestyle of purity.

You may desire a sexually pure lifestyle but feel defeated in that area because sex is a great temptation you cannot overcome. In Second Corinthians 12, Paul talks about the thorn in his flesh that he pleaded with God to take away from him, but God did not take it away. For some of you, the constant desire to have sex is the thorn in your flesh. I want to encourage you with the response God gave to Paul when he was begging for his thorn to be removed. God said, *"My grace is sufficient for you, for my power is made perfect in weakness"* (Second Corinthians 12:9).

After this, Paul decided that he would *"boast all the more gladly of [his] weaknesses, so that the power of Christ may rest upon [him]"* (Second Corinthians 12:9). Your weakness in the area of sex or any other area of your life allows God's power to be perfected. People will know that you cannot obtain sexual purity on your own when you boast about the fact that abstinence is a struggle for you. They will look at your purity journey and marvel at the goodness of God.

This may also encourage them to pursue sexual purity despite their weaknesses as well. Instead of beating yourself up about your shortfalls, take joy in the fact that your weaknesses cause God's power to rest upon you. God will be exalted amidst it all. This is comforting for Christians because they strongly desire to give God glory. If you are weak regarding sexual purity, God can use that. Do not allow your weakness to prevent you from trying or cause you to have a defeatist mentality.

The wait for marriage may seem long and gruesome. I am sure the sexual urges do not help. Isaiah 40:31 encourages us to wait on the Lord. It says, *"But those who wait for the Lord [who expect, look for, and hope in Him] will gain new strength and renew their power; They will lift up their wings [and rise up close to God] like eagles [rising toward the sun]; They will run and not become weary, They will walk and not grow tired."*

God is not a cruel Heavenly Father. He will help you in your waiting season. He will strengthen you and make you powerful during this season. It is my prayer that you make full use of God's free gifts as you wait. I pray that you receive God's strength, power, elevation, endurance, and energy. He promised you these things in His Word.

I would like to end this book with a beautiful promise from God. Lamentations 3:22-23 assures us that *"the faithful love of the*

Lord never ends! His mercies never cease. Great is his faithfulness; his mercies begin afresh each morning." Let these scriptures be an encouragement to you as you pursue a sexually pure lifestyle. Even if your journey is not perfect and you make some mistakes along the way, remember that God's love for you is everlasting, He is faithful, and His mercies are renewed every morning. God has a never-ending supply of love, faithfulness, and mercy for us.

www.ingramcontent.com/pod-product-compliance
Lightning Source LLC
Chambersburg PA
CBHW071753120626
46550CB00002B/770

* 9 7 8 1 9 5 5 5 7 9 1 7 9 *